Rooftop Revolution

Rooftop Revolution

*How Solar Power Can Save
Our Economy—and Our Planet—
from Dirty Energy*

Foreword by **Wesley K. Clark**,
Retired US Army General and NATO's Former
Supreme Allied Commander, Europe

Danny Kennedy

Berrett–Koehler Publishers, Inc.
San Francisco
a BK Currents book

Berrett-Koehler Publishers, Inc.
235 Montgomery Street, Suite 650, San Francisco, CA 94104-2916
Tel: (415) 288-0260   Fax: (415) 362-2512   www.bkconnection.com

Ordering Information

Quantity sales. Special discounts are available on quantity purchases by corporations, associations, and others. For details, contact the "Special Sales Department" at the Berrett-Koehler address above.

Individual sales. Berrett-Koehler publications are available through most bookstores. They can also be ordered directly from Berrett-Koehler: Tel: (800) 929-2929; Fax: (802) 864-7626; www.bkconnection.com.
Orders for college textbook/course adoption use. Please contact Berrett-Koehler: Tel: (800) 929-2929; Fax: (802) 864-7626.
Orders by US trade bookstores and wholesalers. Please contact Ingram Publisher Services, Tel: (800) 509-4887; Fax: (800) 838-1149; E-mail: customer.service@ ingrampublisherservices.com; or visit www.ingrampublisherservices.com/Ordering for details about electronic ordering.

Berrett-Koehler and the BK logo are registered trademarks of Berrett-Koehler Publishers, Inc.

Printed in the United States of America

Berrett-Koehler books are printed on long-lasting acid-free paper. When it is available, we choose paper that has been manufactured by environmentally responsible processes. These may include using trees grown in sustainable forests, incorporating recycled paper, minimizing chlorine in bleaching, or recycling the energy produced at the paper mill.

Library of Congress Cataloging-in-Publication Data
Kennedy, Danny.
    Rooftop revolution : how solar power can save our economy and our planet from dirty energy / Danny Kennedy.
        p. cm.
    Includes bibliographical references and index.
    ISBN 978-1-60994-664-7 (pbk.)
1. Power resources. 2. Solar energy. I. Title.
    HD9502.A2K46 2012
    333.79—dc23
                                                                    2012016962

17   16   15   14   13   12   10 9 8 7 6 5 4 3 2 1

Cover design by Kirk DouPonce, DogEared Design.
Interior design and composition by Gary Palmatier, Ideas to Images.
Elizabeth von Radics, copyeditor; Mike Mollett, proofreader; Medea Minnich, indexer.

To my daughters, Aiko and Ena Jun, and their future children's great-great-great-great-grandchildren.

Contents

Foreword

by General Wesley Clark, US Army (ret.)

THE UNITED STATES TODAY FACES A HISTORIC OPPORTU-
nity—an opportunity every bit as wonderful as Henry Ford's
development of mass production or Thomas Edison's invention
of the light bulb. These economic achievements led to mass
literacy, an acceleration of learning, the creation of the vast
American middle class, and ultimately the suburbanization of
the United States.

Today's opportunity is in the field of clean energy, using the
modern technologies developed since the first energy crisis in
the 1970s to create an America awash in a new prosperity, with
an economy bursting with the most plentiful, accessible, and
least expensive power source in the world. Properly applied,
this energy could spell untold new manufacturing, informa-
tional, and transportation technologies. High-tech industries
and entrepreneurs from all over the world would locate here,
sparking an economic and educational renaissance for the
United States that would catapult us firmly as a role model and
an unquestioned future leader into the twenty-first century.

Danny Kennedy's book, *Rooftop Revolution,* is the story of
the technologies surrounding one of these energy sources: solar
power. He covers in illuminating depth and with jaunty prose
the innovations, economics, and politics of the solar-energy

industry and in so doing provides some deep insight into the challenges and the opportunities facing the United States today.

The challenge of energy is not just a matter of economics, though economics is certainly a part of it. As the nation moved from electric lighting to electric-powered heavy industry and then into the Information Age, and from sweltering summers to ever-present air-conditioning, electricity went from being a luxury to a necessity to a vital foundation for the future. But the nation's supply has not kept pace with either demand or the opportunities ahead.

The utility industry is for the most part heavily regulated, fragmented, and obsolescent in structure and performance. Reliant largely on fossil-fueled steam generation from mammoth plants and a patchwork of wiring called "the grid," the system—if it can even be called that—is inefficient, expensive, stubbornly resistant to modernization, and almost always on the brink of overload and failure. Consumers demand low rates; utility companies, protected usually by public service commissions, fight investments and change; and politicians cater to electoral forces.

Enter the new solar technology—the fastest-developing energy technology today, whose price has fallen dramatically and which promises continued reduction, beyond the point where it will likely be cheaper to add rooftop solar to homes, schools, and factories than to supply them with centrally generated electric power. Indeed it is likely that new generation will be most efficiently managed on a distributed basis and sold into the grid, rather than bought from the grid.

But there are formidable political, regulatory, and bureaucratic obstacles to this vision. And these too are part of Kennedy's story.

On the larger scene, the United States has a dismal legacy of more than 40 years of failure in hammering out a sensible energy strategy, not only for electricity but for liquid fuels as well. Dependent for decades on between 9 million and 12 million barrels of imported fuel, the United States has squandered lives, treasure, and legacy in grasping for foreign-sourced petroleum while sitting on the most abundant energy resources and intellectual and entrepreneurial capital in the world.

Three wars, some 7,000 US military deaths, and several trillion dollars spent on conflict, military presence, and fuel imports attest to our failure. Companies that once employed proud and stalwart US citizens are now funnels channeling US fuel expenditures to foreign dictators and others whose governments benefit in direct proportion to America's economic pain. And in the process, they are agents of distortion of US strategy and policy, conveying a false sense of the real challenges and opportunities facing us in the future and reinforcing their own commercial interests with the most powerful accumulation of wealth in the world.

In less than two presidential terms, with scarcely any expenditure of US government monies, the United States could be energy independent. The "gold rush" in North Dakota today, as thousands of workers pour into the state seeking lucrative jobs in the new oil sector, powered by private investment, indicates the hunger for energy and the drive to satiate it.

But we also must take seriously the rising carbon content in the atmosphere and the even more dangerous buildup of other greenhouse gases like methane. So, while using energy independence as a rallying cry to jump-start the economy, we have to simultaneously transition away from fossil fuels—no easy task with a trillion-dollar inventory of liquid-fueled private automobiles. And the electricity that powers them must be renewably generated rather than drawn from fossilized carbon. But, again, we have the technology to do this.

Rooftop
Revolution

An Energy Primer

Let there be light.

—GENESIS 1:3

WE LIVE IN ELECTRICITY LIKE A FISH LIVES IN WATER. UNTIL a big storm knocks out our power or we blow a fuse by using the microwave and the blender at the same time, most of us don't think a whole lot about the electricity that surrounds us and powers our modern lives. We pay a monthly bill—usually while grumbling about its expense—and our lights stay lit, our toast gets toasted, and our web extends worldwide. Beyond that? Well, we may have a notion that Benjamin Franklin discovered electricity while flying a kite in a storm (that's a myth, actually—Franklin may have never flown that kite, though he did do important research into how electricity is conducted). We may have an idea that a few big—and not necessarily benevolent—corporations have a monopoly on our power supply. And we've likely heard that the way we currently supply our homes with precious electricity is damaging our environment and endangering our nation's security.

Yet we haven't heard much about viable alternatives to this status quo, so we keep paying that monthly bill. We get on-demand light, heat, refrigeration, entertainment, information, blended margaritas, and microwaved pizza. And those corporations keep lining their pockets while our nation and our world are put in an ever-more-precarious situation.

What if I told you that there *is* a viable alternative—despite what Dirty Energy propagandists would have you believe? There's a way to power your home that saves you money, that can free our nation from dependence on foreign energy sources, and that's completely renewable. It's ready and available right now.

It's an American invention called solar power. And the ascent of solar—following a Rooftop Revolution—is set to remake our world. To be certain, it's fighting against some monumental institutions and deeply ingrained behaviors and mind-sets. (If you're thinking, *Oh, solar—it's just a fantasy some radicals had in the 1970s,* the Dirty Energy public relations [PR] machine has gotten into your head!) But recent advances of ingenuity based on solar power's brilliance have unleashed the creativity of entrepreneurs and capital. These advances are supported by serious social movements—committed activists who seek to break the corporate power of Big Oil and Big Coal and to reduce pollution and corruption. In this book I explain the early history of the Rooftop Revolution as well as what needs to happen next and how you can join the fight.

Electricity 101

We *already* get our energy from the sun—we just do it in the most laughably inefficient way imaginable. In short, fossil fuels—that is, coal, oil, and natural gas—*are* the sun's energy, stored in the form of 200-million-year-old plants and extracted today by dangerous, costly, environment-destroying methods.

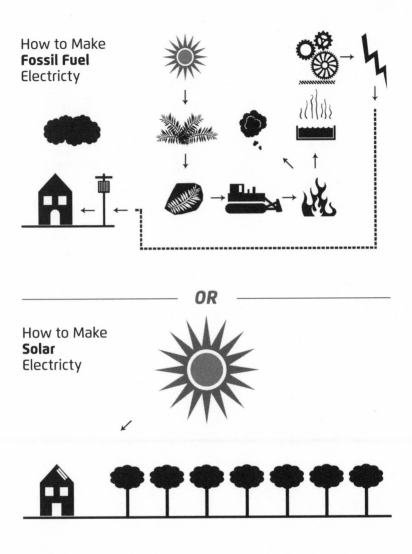

How to Make
Fossil Fuel
Electricty

OR

How to Make
Solar
Electricty

Solar power, by contrast, comes directly from the source. There are no mines and no rigs—a solar panel just sits in the sun, takes in sunlight, and turns that light into electricity right at the point of use. There's no costly and unsightly transportation, no danger of explosion or mine collapse, no mountaintop removal, no Fukushima or Deepwater Horizon, and no spilling or killing required. Just clean, cheap energy.

You don't have to be an energy expert to see how strong the case for solar power is. I've spent my adult life fighting on the front lines of the Rooftop Revolution, working around, with, and often in spite of the energy industry, yet I have no formal training as an electrical engineer. So I can tell you, in layperson's terms, what you need to know before joining this fight.

How did electricity become ubiquitous and affordable for most Americans?

The machines that make the electricity became standardized, and the businesses that delivered them scaled. The machine most commonly used to make electricity in the United States and elsewhere is the steam turbine, developed by a British engineer in the 1880s, which extracts thermal energy from pressurized steam. That pressurized steam is created by boiling water, which is heated by burning various forms of fossil fuels. We get those fossil fuels in a variety of ways: open pit mines, shaft mines, drilling rigs on land and sea, and "fracking"—or geologic fracturing—which is the propagation of fractures in a rock layer by pumping high-pressure liquid down a hole to release natural gas locked in the sediments and fissures.

All of these aforementioned fuels store energy in chemical bonds; the energy is released when they're burned. The energy got there hundreds of millions of years ago, when these fuels were plants, through the process of photosynthesis: the sun put that energy there. Most of the world's coal, for instance, comes from the fossilized remains of dinosaur-era plants, hence the term *fossil fuel.*

See what I mean about a "laughably inefficient way" to get power from the sun?

Coal is mined from holes in the ground—often from shafts but increasingly, due to the use of machinery, from open pits. Humans have been extracting coal from shaft mines for nearly a millennium—and it's a hugely dangerous enterprise, as you often hear about in the news. Every year thousands die in mine disasters, especially in China, as that country slakes its thirst for low-cost coal. Aside from the human costs, mining has well-known environmental repercussions, such as water pollution, mountain-top removal, and forest clear cutting.

Sucking oil and gas—fossil fuels in liquid or gaseous form—from beneath the ground is a similarly invasive process. While the hole in the ground isn't usually as large as the holes caused by mines, the cumulative impact of a drilling field can be quite extensive. I spent a year documenting one such project in Papua New Guinea for an academic thesis in human geography, and it took me the better part of two months just to walk around the drill sites that fed one pipeline in the mountains near Lake Kutubu, the second-largest high-altitude lake in the world. I saw firsthand the spills, helicopter accidents, invasive logging, and other ecological effects that made this "best in breed" oil project pretty high impact. Offshore rigs are similarly dangerous, as we recently saw in BP's devastating oil spill in the Gulf of Mexico.

Gas drilling is a little different. It requires a large industrial infrastructure nearby to liquefy or pressurize the gas for transport in some form. A new gas project off Australia's northwest coast has so far cost $40 billion just to get up and running. In the United States and elsewhere, getting to natural gas increasingly requires fracking, which is quite controversial because the liquids used are frequently toxic and because the volumes of fluids injected underground are causing groundwater contamination and even earthquakes. We all know that mining and drilling are pretty ugly, but we rarely make the connection between this ugliness and that little light that comes on every time we open the fridge.

Perhaps the biggest problem that we inadvertently exacerbate when we use electricity is climate change (or global warming, as it's also called): when fossil fuels release the energy locked in chemical-based bonds from plants that once captured carbon dioxide, they also release some of that carbon dioxide into the atmosphere. The way we currently create and process energy releases much of this carbon dioxide pollution. Many books have been written about the subject of climate change, and this is not one of them. Every relevant, reputable scientist in the field has shown that the way we currently create and process energy is a cause of climate change. If we don't slow the steady rise of global warming, our planet will be beset by more drought, more floods, more hunger, more disease, and more-extreme weather as time progresses. Even if we could clean up all the pollution or accept all the other impacts of the fossil-fuel-extraction industry, we can't afford to accept the worsening of climate change that burning these fuels causes.

Then there are nukes. A nuclear power plant uses radiation from uranium, instead of fossil fuels, to boil water and create the steam for its steam turbines. The problems with nukes are many, from uranium mining to nuclear waste, which can kill many things living nearby for generations—think of the Chernobyl and Fukushima nuclear disasters—and because of these risks, new nuclear plants are virtually uninsurable (that is, expensive)!

It's worth noting that turbines can be powered by forces other than steam, the most common being hydroelectric turbines, which capture and transmit the kinetic energy of falling water. Similarly, wind turbines use the power of naturally occurring wind to create energy, which is also sneakily due to the sun's heating parts of the atmosphere, changing pressure, and causing wind. Like solar, wind is a wonderfully clean and renewable energy source.

The Grid

The system of wires between these electricity-generating machines and the users of that electricity is known as "the grid." There are basically two types of wires in the grid. Electricity begins its journey at the types of generators we've just discussed (which are usually far from high-population areas). It's carried on high-voltage transmission wires to "demand centers," where transformers reduce the electricity's voltage and send it out via distribution lines to consumers.

Electricity is a vital commodity service that powers our economy. We're the end users in our homes and offices, and we pay the full retail rate for dirty electricity. A big commercial user—like a factory, a store, or a university—may pay a lower rate, and some industrial users negotiate to buy electricity almost at wholesale prices. This pricing pyramid of lower-cost bulk buying and higher-cost structures for residential and other users has been applied in the United States and many other countries for much of the past century. In China, however, it's different: to create efficiency in bulk use, China's utilities charge higher prices, but they ask retail users to pay less because they aim to spread the benefits of electricity to more citizens.

The grid's complexity has grown over time. The fundamental structure is often described as "hub and spoke"—central-station generators being surrounded by wires out to users—but it's more like a hub and spaghetti and meatballs, with more and more generators also on the rim and a crisscross of wires around the network.

Managing the grid is challenging. The technology supporting it is one matter, but then consider the interests of the businesses generating the power and maintaining the grid, and then think of the rights of consumers, who are represented by politically appointed regulators of those businesses—and you start to see how the grid is actually a very tangled web!

Nonetheless creating the grid—and thereby providing the service of electricity to a nation of consumers—was one of the great achievements of the twentieth century in the United States. Although nearly 90 percent of urban dwellers had electricity by the 1930s, only 10 percent of rural dwellers did. Private energy companies argued that providing electricity to rural farmers was too expensive (and they charged farmers up to four times more than they charged city dwellers). As part of the New Deal, the Rural Electrification Administration brought the productivity and the personal improvements afforded by electricity to the many farmers who were going without.

Today countries are still judged by their ability to deliver electricity service to more and more people, although a lot of people are still off the grid. At least 1 billion people can't take electricity for granted; in fact, they've probably never experienced it, but they're likely to in the coming decade as new, more-localized ways of making electricity become commonplace. Their governments—in India and some African countries, for example—are trying to not re-create the brittle twentieth-century model but rather have a more flexible set of resources to serve their communities with electricity. This is actually more reliable and secure; here in the United States, our grid is at risk of breakdown (if a tree falls on a power line, it can trigger the collapse of a whole network as much of the Northeast experienced in 2003) and attack (the grid's many linkages make it an easy target for terrorists).

One of the resources being deployed in these countries without extensive grids, as they seek to leapfrog the era of dirty-electricity supply built around the expensive and insecure central-station model, is solar power. Places like Germany, India, Japan, and California have also been in the forefront of the Rooftop Revolution as they have connected solar panels to their grids to augment their power supplies; we'll visit some of these places in later chapters.

Shining a Light on Solar

Solar power is harnessed in a number of ways, including some solar-thermal solutions that concentrate sunlight directly onto water-filled vessels—to boil water, generate steam, and spin a turbine much like the fossil-fuel-based electricity technologies. There are also straight solar hot-water systems, which heat our water only for direct use—not to create electricity—and are very efficient ways to create hot-water service.

But the solar power that I most want to focus on—because it's the real game changer—is what's known as *photovoltaics,* a method of generating electric power by converting solar radiation (*photo*) into direct-current electricity (*voltaic*) using semiconductors. When people talk about solar panels, they're talking about this technology, though the systems range in size, from one small cell (for instance, to power a single light in Zambia) to 10 panels (to power a home in California) to 400,000 panels (to power a city in Crimea).

Solar panels are often called *modules* because they can be customized to serve any size electricity demand. This alone

makes them a remarkably disruptive technology to the electricity industry. Better yet, they don't require fuel or produce pollution. The *production* of the panels may cause some pollution, as
the production of any manufactured goods does, but it's minuscule compared with the production of fossil fuels, and it can
be contained in a closed production process. Plus, solar-panel
components are completely recyclable—something fossil-fuel
industries can't claim about their products—and they pay back
the energy put into them in the first few years of operation.

A solar panel at work is like magic in the sense Arthur C.
Clarke meant when he said, "Any sufficiently advanced technology is indistinguishable from magic." Here we have light shining
on the surface of the silicon cells, creating an electric current;
it's a tiny amount, but sometimes that's enough. For instance,
there's my wristwatch, which I've had for nearly a decade and
have never had to wind or replace a battery. It has a tiny amount
of photovoltaic silicon on its face, and that provides the power
for the mechanism day in and day out. The minuscule current of
electricity that this cell makes can be joined with currents from
a series of silicon cells that make up a solar panel, which in turn
can be strung together to form an even bigger flow of electricity.

When you hear energy experts talk about "loads," they're
referring to electricity usage. Solar panels can be quite close
to loads and sized appropriately. This is different from steam-
based technologies, which tend to be far from loads and over-
sized, so they're sure to meet demand. Solar power is not only
clean but also local. And now it's the most cost-effective.

Before we proceed, I should explain how we measure power
and energy: "Power" is what we can directly use, like the water
we pour into our mouths. "Energy" is like all the water stored up
in the clouds; it has the potential to come down to us, but until

and unless it does we may go thirsty. That is to say, we can have energy but not necessarily usable power. Power is measured in *kilowatts,* and electricity comes in *kilowatt-hours* because we're measuring how long a source can provide an amount of power. Your electricity bill charges you per kilowatt-hour.

The energy potential in 20 days of sunshine falling on Earth is the same as that of all the coal, oil, and natural gas known to humans. We may find more fossil fuels at some point, but solar power is effectively infinite, unlike fossil fuels, which someday, especially at the rate we're using them, *will* run out. They are governed by the reality of scarcity and become more expensive the more you use them. Sunshine as fuel renews every day. It is abundant and becomes cheaper the more you use it. I admit that there's an assumption here—that the sun will rise and shine on us—but the day it doesn't, we'll have bigger issues to deal with than whether the toaster's working!

So if you understand the significant potential of solar energy, you're going to be excited about the reality of solar panels to tap it. They take 15 percent of sunlight's energy and convert it into useable power. And solar panels are more affordable and more powerful each year. These 2-by-3-foot framed modules of glass and aluminum, sandwiching some slices of silicon arrayed in a 60- or 72-cell format, and the economy that will emerge as part and parcel of them have the potential to completely negate the entire grid infrastructure built around steam turbines since the end of the nineteenth century.

The grid, as it exists now, consists of large generators that convert the energy stored in fossil fuels into electricity that's then sent over cables and wires into our homes and businesses. We're dumb recipients down a one-way line. The growing demand for electricity, plus constraints on transmission systems and the environmental costs of fossil fuels, has resulted in many concerns about the limits to this approach among politicians and others hoping to keep the lights on. Solar technology allows individuals to become producers of power, too, and to engage in the creation of the electricity they use.

This shift has been described as enabling electricity users to become "prosumers"—producer-consumers—on a smart grid, a bit like the Internet has allowed individuals to not simply consume media content but also create and share it. It need not be a frightening transition to be more involved in energy production while we consume it. Society just needs businesses that make doing so seamless and simple—and maybe a little sexy. The economics can already make it worth our while.

I call this change from dirty-energy dependency to a portfolio of clean, distributed energy solutions the *Solar Ascent* because solar will be the primary source of power. This transition will be triggered by this decade's Rooftop Revolution, in which many millions take part in the Solar Ascent by producing their own power on their own places. In other words, the longer-term evolution will be driven by mass adoption of solar panels on our rooftops in a historic burst of resistance to the powers that be.

The previous big energy revolution was the Industrial Revolution. Coal combined with the power of steam engines created new opportunities in our economy and changed the world. Replacing our agricultural society (before the steam engine, most work was fueled by eating plants with their more freshly stored sunlight) with an industrial society unleashed a boom in productivity and innovation that has lasted for centuries. The Rooftop Revolution will launch similarly world-changing outcomes if it succeeds. If it doesn't, we'll be stuck with the impacts of the dirty-energy sources that steam power bequeathed to us.

Join the Revolution

Making solar power easier to access, demonstrating solar's power by adopting it into your life, becoming involved in spreading sunshine into other people's lives with electricity cost savings and a reduction in pollution, voting for positive energy policies (or those that break the grip of fossil fuels and support the emergence of solar and other local, clean energy)—all are things we must accomplish now. Speaking truth to power, in the form of government and corporate bureaucrats beholden to what I've learned to call "King CONG" (the four-headed monster of coal, oil, nukes, and gas) is also critical.

So get involved. Use this book as a resource and a how-to guide, not just to putting solar on your roof but also to being part of the fight against Dirty Energy. (Of course, if you're ready to put solar on your roof, do that too!) Right now it's important that everyone know the truth about solar's power and how we should be making energy. Our future—our safety, our prosperity, and our environment—depends on the success of the Rooftop Revolution.

In each chapter of this book is a section called "What You Can Do as a Rooftop Revolutionary" (in the short term and in the long term) and where you can learn more.

The Rooftop Revolution has begun. The time to fight is now. *Semper ad lucem*—always toward the light!

What You Can Do as a Rooftop Revolutionary

▶ You have taken the first step to join the Rooftop Revolution by reading this prologue and educating yourself about how electricity is produced. Now take that knowledge a step further: read your electricity bill thoroughly and gain a strong understanding of the charges.

▶ Ask your friends and colleagues if they understand how electricity is produced. If they don't have a good grasp, fill in the blanks for them.

CHAPTER 1

Sunny Side Up

Now, here, you see, it takes all the running you can do,
to keep in the same place. If you want to get somewhere
else, you must run at least twice as fast as that!

—LEWIS CARROLL, FROM *THROUGH THE LOOKING GLASS*

SOLAR IS DEAD—AT LEAST THAT'S WHAT ITS DETRACTORS want you to believe. Dead in the water, they say, dead as disco and dinosaurs, a hippie-dippy pipe dream gone up in smoke. But these solar-energy opponents, many of whom hail from the coal, oil, nuke, and gas lobbies (ol' King CONG), have recently been pointing to just one example in their efforts to prove their point: Solyndra, the erstwhile solar-industry poster child, which, in 2011, made headlines and drew nationwide derision when it went bankrupt after receiving a $500 million loan from the US government.

But here's the truth King CONG doesn't want you to know: The downfall of Solyndra actually proved that solar power is fast becoming the most cost-effective and efficient form of electricity on Earth. The company's failure was largely due to competition in a market that's been growing at an amazing rate, and Solyndra's idea for a lower-cost solar module (which had a daft cylindrical design that was too fragile and too expensive to make) simply couldn't compete with less-expensive, mass-produced silicon-based solar panels, the cheapest of which largely come from China—not an uncommon practice as new products become more common and affordable.

Solar-panel manufacturing is relatively simple (it's less complex than, say, making a car), and a lot of it can be done using automated methods or low-skilled labor, of which China has plenty.

Let's look at Apple Inc. for a moment. Here's a company that designs its devices in California and then sells them through clever online and physical retail stores around the world, but it manufactures these products in Chinese factories. The world loves Apple products, and Wall Street loves the company, which in 2012 surpassed Exxon as the most valuable in the world. It currently has more cash than the US government! There are problems aplenty with this model of manufacturing, and I'm not naïve about the issues—such as labor conditions for the factory workers and environmental impacts like the pollution caused by poor regulation—but let's be realistic: Apple is traveling a well-worn path, following such companies as Dell and General Electric. That path leads to great opportunity in ancillary businesses—the benefits created by Apple in creativity, publishing, recording, telephony, and sales of its various devices are legend—and the greater good, which is the availability of Apple's amazing products.

The truth is, we should be glad that China is making solar panels cheaply—it makes these products more affordable for Americans and the billion-plus people on the planet who don't currently get electricity and would otherwise turn to dirty planet-cooking coal, oil, or gas to get it. Though domestic manufacturing of solar panels and solar-panel parts is gaining strength in America over the first decade of the twenty-first century, the real jobs and margins right now are elsewhere in the industry—in sales, marketing, finance, and the installation of these products. Most of the jobs are downstream.

So Solyndra went bust, which is sad for the people who worked there, but its demise in no way marks the end of an entire industry. Nevertheless many people who had turned a blind eye to government pork for bad ideas and bankruptcies waiting to happen, and those who had sought federal funding for all sorts of less-worthy ventures, like a bridge in Alaska that went nowhere, had a field day. There was a frenzy of media coverage fed by political hearings and witch hunts that made this one company's fate one of the biggest stories of the year. Indeed, the hysteria surrounding Solyndra's bankruptcy reminds me of the people who thought that the fall of the web browser Netscape marked the end of the Internet. More column inches were devoted to the Solyndra story in most outlets than to Japan's Fukushima nuclear-power-plant disaster, which wrote down the Tokyo Electric Power Company's value by $13 billion and required a $9 billion bailout by the people of Japan.

But why has the so-called demise of solar energy and the solar industry been so widely reported? Because the rise of solar power is a direct threat to the rich and powerful corporations that create electricity through dirty, unsustainable, and harmful fossil fuel.

The Battle for America's Head and Heart

There's an epic struggle afoot for the head and the heart of America. And the fat cats in Dirty Energy who feed off our addiction to fossil fuel have an obvious motivation—profits—to keep us in denial about our bad habit. They don't want us to dwell on our energy addiction and the damage it does to ourselves, our planet, and our children's future. So Dirty Energy dips into its very deep pockets to tout its brand of power in the news and keep America in the dark about cleaner, smarter, more-affordable options out there. But as a growing number of Americans are finding out, they do have options.

Although change is difficult and requires traction, it's easier when someone shines a light on the path ahead, and this is what the solar-power movement is doing: providing a solution, an alternative to business as usual, while the coal, oil, nuke, and gas giants continue their fight for the status quo. Not to be too highfalutin, but when the colonial Americans were frustrated by heavy taxation without government representation, it wasn't until they saw a new direction—inspired by the French Republic's demand for liberty—that forces of change pushed them to have their own revolution.

It's time for a new revolution, an energy revolution, *our* revolution—a Rooftop Revolution. The movement worldwide to go solar—to usurp the powers that be in our existing electricity grids and put power in the hands of those in the developing world who don't have it—is creating a space for as profound a change. Breaking up monopolies, spreading benefits to the poorest, making consumers producers, and getting polluters to pay and thus using market forces to get them to participate in building a clean economy—this is what the Rooftop Revolution is all about. And that's why it's not surprising that King CONG is fighting back.

In 2012 oil barons such as the Koch brothers will spend many millions on TV ad campaigns to tar President Barack Obama with the same brush they used on Solyndra. Those who have the most to lose, the opponents of solar, will come out with fists flying—as the US Chamber of Commerce did in the 2010 election cycle. The massive business lobby outspent the Republican and Democratic National Committees combined to further its official policy of digging up every last ounce of fuel in the ground and burning it as soon as possible.

We need to urge our politicians to refuse money from energy companies and their lobbies so that our representatives can make decisions about energy policy without being beholden to paymasters and without ignoring the public demand for clean, local energy. And public opinion is clear: according to the SCHOTT Solar Barometer, when voters were asked to select an energy source they would financially support if they were in charge of US energy policy, 39 percent said they would choose solar power while a measly 3 percent chose coal—almost the inverse ratio of our representatives in Congress.

Mark my words, we'll have to battle a lot more of this malarkey in the near future. Case in point: the viral campaign that the American Petroleum Institute (API), the powerful oil and natural-gas trade association, launched in January 2012. Dubbed "Vote 4 Energy," it was scripted by industry executives in a big election year to dupe viewers into believing that the tired and traditional use of dirty energy would somehow lead our country back to prosperity. Greenpeace, the environmental advocacy organization, released a parody video that exposed the reality that the API campaign wasn't divulging—that these energy sources are damaging and unsustainable and that the jobs the corporations claim to create are only temporary. But which ads do you think more Americans see—ads funded by incredibly rich oil corporations or those of a nonprofit? The API campaign included radio, television, and print advertising in election-year swing states, including Ohio, Pennsylvania, and

Virginia—fertile ground for political theater in which energy is a key issue.

As the API's spokesman said when launching Vote 4 Energy, "It's not about candidates, it's not about political parties, it's not even about political philosophy. Energy should not be a partisan issue. . . . We believe a vote for energy will elevate the energy conversation." I wholeheartedly agree with the API that energy isn't, or shouldn't be, attached to a political party or philosophy. We know, however, that these politicized battles are not always elevated into some erudite discourse but rather end up in the gutter of half-truths and name-calling. (You know we've reached a new low when "Drill, baby, drill" is the apex of political rhetoric.) We know that the incumbent industries present our energy options subjectively, as the Vote 4 Energy campaign shows, and that the clean-energy industry is coming to this gunfight armed with a couple of slingshots.

The Public Demand for Clean, Local Energy

Whether Americans will see through King CONG's smoke and mirrors and clever communications is another question. We have to take this battle seriously because CONG and its industry associations could hamper our momentum in bringing what our country needs and what an ever-growing number of our citizens want: clean, local energy. CONG intends its long and sustained campaign to frame solar as at best some "future technology" and at worst a total failure. Nothing could be further from the truth: solar power is ready right now. It's what all the satellites in space use to operate, beaming bits and bytes of data down to Earth for our communications and entertainment. And there are new advances in solar technology every day.

More importantly, millions of people globally are now using solar power in their homes. With the advent of creative customer finance solutions, more US businesses and households became solar-power plants for themselves in the past 10 years than in the previous three decades. One of the best competitors of the company I helped found, Sungevity, just launched SolarStrong, a billion-dollar program with the US military and Bank of America to put solar panels on the homes of 300,000 US servicemen and -women—almost doubling the solar-home stock in America within five years.

Solar cells, a high-performance technology set, produce electricity that each year costs less and less compared with electricity derived from coal, oil, nukes, and gas, which costs more each year. Before long we could all live in a country that's largely powered by solar panels on the skins of our buildings and the surfaces of our vacant lands—and maybe even on the surfaces of our roads.

Lest you think I and my fellow solar entrepreneurs are biased because we've helped build businesses in this space, here are some hard numbers from the US Energy Information Administration from around the same time some pundits were striking up the band to play the dirge for the solar industry: US solar-generated electricity expanded in 2011 by 45 percent over the first three quarters of 2010. In comparison, natural-gas electrical generation rose only 1.6 percent, while nuclear output declined by 2.8 percent and coal-generated electricity dropped by 4.2 percent.

Solar is on the rise across the United States. In 2010, 16 states installed more than enough to supply approximately 2,000 homes, compared with only four states in 2007. California saw huge increases in usage, crossing the head-spinning 1-gigawatt marker on solar rooftops—a level only five countries have achieved. (To put this number into perspective, 1 gigawatt is the capacity of a whole nuclear power plant, which could power 200,000 homes!) But that's just a start for this form of power generated from solar panels.

Worldwide the solar industry is also taking off in a big way: China enjoyed such a burst of solar power that it recalibrated the target in its twelfth five-year plan to 15 gigawatts installed by 2015—50 percent higher than the previous target and 50 percent more than we expect to have in the United States.

The big surprise to me personally, as someone in the solar business, is that China caught up to the United States in installed solar panels in 2011, which I had not expected to happen for years. Five years earlier there were almost none in all of China—and the United States had a 50-year head start.

On the subcontinent, Pakistan has passed the point where solar power is cheaper than a lot of electricity that comes from diesel generators, and India is upping its target from 20 to 33 gigawatts to be installed by 2020.

Germany produced more than 18 billion kilowatt-hours of solar electricity in 2011. That's 60 percent more than it produced the year before and is enough to supply 5 million households for a year. In December 2011 the country installed 3 gigawatts of solar panels in just one month—enough capacity to power 600,000 homes!

By any measure, the world is experiencing a solar boom. Momentum is building, and we have to keep it going for the benefit of our economy and our planet's longevity. To do that we have to combat Dirty Energy's efforts with our own, and the time is now.

A Perversion of Power

Now more than ever it is critical that we set the record straight on energy use in the United States—to tell the truth about the progression of solar energy and to present the facts that the mainstream media has largely ignored or underreported: that fossil fuel is the real dinosaur in the energy industry and that much of the world is seeing the light about solar power. We must get our elected officials to recognize the true value of solar power and to embrace the opportunity to build on this clean form of electricity generation and spawn a new breed of entrepreneurs and businesses that will employ millions and pull us out of dark times.

The Solar Ascent is kicking in around the globe, and we need to be leaders of this movement. Our next step is to clear from our heads the fog of misinformation from the fossil-fuel industry, assess the landscape clearly, and urge others to do so, as well. This means getting our friends in the news media to start reporting facts on *all* sides of the energy debate.

Working in the solar industry in the months following the Solyndra scandal at the end of 2011 really felt like slipping through the looking glass into a crazy, upside-down world. I'd been working with others for about a decade to realize solar's potential. Sungevity, the company I'd helped build, had just doubled in size and we'd had a banner year, as had most of our competitors, selling solar solutions to mainstream Americans. Yet in the months following Solyndra's crash, from Thanksgiving to the New Year, everyone started worrying that we wouldn't make it. "Sorry about that solar thing"; "Shame it didn't work out," they'd say, or, "Would've been nice to have clean energy."

What the hell is up? I was thinking. *We're winning!* Solar is
the fastest-growing source of energy on Earth because it's the
only source of energy whose costs are declining rapidly. All the
others, including natural gas, are going up in price—no matter
what the gas industry says. Although there is *currently* a surplus
of natural gas in the US market due to the lower cost of fracking,
it won't last because when you're dealing with a finite energy
source and consuming it in the vast amounts that Americans
do, it's impossible to keep costs low over the long term. And
no matter how much the industry touts the wonders of fracking, when its technology causes earthquakes—as fracking did
in March 2011 in Youngstown, Ohio—costs and other ramifica-
tions are sure to mount.

On the other hand, sustainable solar energy is swiftly
becoming earth-shattering in much more figurative and economically beneficial ways. Solar prices are coming down; and if
we stay the course we're on, they'll continue to drop. Globally,
solar is the fastest-growing industry, valued at more than $100
billion. And in the United States, it's the fastest-growing job-
creating sector. Solar grew nearly 7 percent as an employment
generator while the economy flatlined—a tenth of that growth
from August 2010 to 2011. Things are good, and they're getting
better. The solar industry is admittedly still just under 1 percent
of the whole energy picture, but it's growing fast. Solar is David
against King CONG's Goliath, but we're armed with a mighty,
badass, solar-powered slingshot. As my Aussie friends like to
say, "From little things, big things grow."

And what are some of these "big things"? For starters, the
cold hard cash being pumped into the industry is where the smart
money is going. Just before Christmas 2011, Google invested $94
million in four large-scale solar photovoltaic projects, edging

the total amount the search giant invested in clean-energy projects toward $900 million. Not to be beaten, and always one to place a bet when assets are artificially depressed, investment guru Warren Buffett dropped almost $2 billion on California's Topaz Solar Farm, which will sell solar electricity to Pacific Gas and Electric (PG&E), the local utility company, and generate electricity for about 160,000 homes. Globally, investment in renewable energy was up to $260 billion, from $243 billion in 2010 and $186.5 billion in 2009. Solar got half of that. Indeed Bloomberg New Energy Finance recorded the trillionth dollar of investment in clean energy since its records started in 2004.

So, though the Solyndra scandal was the big solar-energy industry newsmaker in 2011, several more-significant events point to the globe's movement from dirty, centralized electricity production to clean, local power. Some of them were as significant as a sea change, though the weatherpeople in the mass media may not have spotted them, one being the economic aftermath of Japan's devastating 2011 earthquake and subsequent tsunami, which caused a meltdown at the country's Fukushima nuclear power plant. This proof of the risks of nuclear power drove yet another nail into the coffin of nuclear energy in the United States.

Nukes are all but done here because what banker today could legitimately finance a nuclear power plant? No one will finance one unless the money comes from socialized governments willing to take on the risks with public funds. I'm not saying nukes are *completely* dead; in February 2012 Southern Company, an electricity generator, announced plans to build two nuclear plants in Georgia, but this construction is possible only because it is being prepaid by consumers at the rate of $3 per month. This mandatory way of capitalizing the plants will be augmented by Department of Energy loan guarantees that are 20 times what Solyndra got. The point is really that one of the biggest pieces of financial news that has yet to be clearly reported is that there's little chance that new nukes can compete with clean electricity from solar panels.

At the same time that the media was missing this big shift in the markets away from a nuclear renaissance, reports showed that major economies throughout the world were moving to clean-energy sources, but this trend was rarely addressed in mainstream outlets. For every negative Solyndragate scoop, there should have been three times as many stories on how advanced economies were getting their juice.

Germany now gets a whopping 20 percent of its power from clean, sustainable energy, including solar power, and the country has become a laboratory for the kind of electricity supply that the world will benefit from in years to come. At age 41 I'm old enough to remember when fossil-fuel industry-sponsored experts told us that no more than 5 percent of the electricity grid could possibly come from renewable—so-called intermittent—resources. Then, when innovative people pushed the envelope, the numbers were raised to 10 percent and then to 15 percent. Now in Germany—one of Europe's few strong economies—more than 25 percent of energy comes in the form of wind and solar electrons on many days. The rest of Europe didn't want the Germans to hog the solar spotlight, and now many other places have at times adopted a higher density of clean electricity in their grid than even Germany—such as Denmark (more than 30 percent), Spain (35 percent), and Portugal (50 percent). Italy installed more than enough solar power for a million homes in 2011, despite its fiscal worries.

In Crimea, Ukraine, a Vienna-based developer, Activ Solar, built the world's largest solar park, a project of more than 100 megawatts in capacity—one-tenth the size of a nuke—and worth about 300 million euros (US $387 million), according to reports. The Perova plant consists of 440,000 solar panels, spans 500 hundred acres, and will generate enough peak-load power for the electrical needs for all of Simferopol, Crimea's capital.

And what do these nations get through the adoption of clean energy? Not blackouts and higher electricity bills but rather employment and price stability. Germany in particular has benefitted from this, creating hundreds of thousands of jobs, becoming a center of excellence for the export of high-tech products, and providing lower-cost electricity for its population than energy that comes out of the conventional grid—all while shutting down the bulk of its nuclear-power-plant fleet.

In spite of the staggering advances Germany has made, politics is besieging it. The country is experiencing a backlash against renewable energy, led by fiscal conservatives in the German parliament who believe that the incentives for solar power will cost too much in the future. The debate is sure to wax and wane, and even at this high-tide mark there's going to be some flux. Although the conservatives are reducing the rate of payments for solar power, the benefits of solar incentives have already taken effect, and the German population understands this. More people support it politically because they're making money from the shift. So no matter what changes the Bundestag wants to make, there's no turning back.

The German economy is on a positive path. The country is moving from boiling water with stored-solar-power supplies to getting electricity by other sustainable and economically beneficial means. More importantly, 50 percent of Germany's solar panels are owned by individuals and farms, not big corporate generators. As one writer put it, this is a good thing: "Decentralized power generation, more relocalization and reregionalization of economic activity, the world is getting smaller while more connected and therefore in a way bigger at the same time."

Poised for Progress

While these groundbreaking shifts have been taking place in Europe, China, and the United States, the world's reigning superpowers have brought about important changes of global significance in the electricity market. The year 2011 marked the first time in history that these powerhouses invested more money in renewable energy than in fossil fuels. The main driver of this has been the fact that solar power has fallen in price to be equal to, or even less than, much of the electricity we pay for in our current grid.

In California, one of the nation's most expensive electricity markets, a homeowner's peak electricity use, on average, cost more than $0.18 per kilowatt-hour in 2011 and went as high as $0.35 per kilowatt-hour. Solar-leasing companies save the average consumer more than 15 percent, depending on the cost of installation and financing. Every state is different, but the economics are improving all the time, and by 2015, according to projections by the Department of Energy, two-thirds of US households will save money by using solar electricity.

The main driver of the cost reduction in installed solar panels is the fact that the core component of solar-power systems—the silicon cell—is, as we've discussed, now being produced in volume. We've seen this happen before in the computer hardware industry with the commoditization of the silicon chip, a

THE PRICE OF ELECTRICITY
Made from Solar or Fossil Fuels

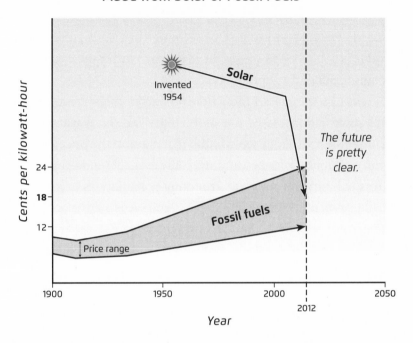

slightly different-sized product but surprisingly similar from a manufacturing point of view. As integrated circuits or semiconductors became much cheaper, microprocessing—the service they provide—became more widely available for less, and microprocessors ended up in everything from cars to phones. Like silicon chips, solar cells continue to drop in cost and become more powerful as time goes by.

This is incredible news for people and the planet. Solar panels are now being mass produced, and consumers are benefiting from cost reduction due to volume production, much like with cell phones and other electronics. For every doubling of the manufacturing capacity of solar panels, there's been an 18 percent price reduction of the end product. The investments made in solar-product manufacturing by China, Korea, India, Germany, the United States, and other countries over the past five years have broadly tripled the production capacity, bringing down the end-product price more than 50 percent. That value is passed on to you in the price you pay for the electricity coming out of these products.

Just as the mass production of silicon chips drove down the price and increased the affordability and the availability of computing power, so too will the reduction in the price of silicon cells make solar power universally available and affordable. This will unleash an era of economic possibility as to how we can use solar power, which, today, some say is silly. Who knew that your oven or clothes dryer might serve you better with a microprocessor? Similarly, a self-powered solar cell phone or a case that charges your laptop will be something we can have in the near future. To some degree, you can choose your own solar adventure, for the solar-powered future is at hand.

But don't think this all will come easily and without lots of metaphorical blood, sweat, and tears. We can't be complacent and wait for it to happen, for as far into the woods as we've traveled chasing our societal fossil-fuel addiction is as far out as we have to walk toward the sun. To win the energy battle, we need to organize, get solar on our homes, and demand positive energy policies. We solar citizens must stand up and be counted, as do the people employed in the industry and all of those who want to pursue the many commercial opportunities that low-cost solar makes possible. Spawning easy and affordable solutions for low-cost solar hardware will take lots of genius, human hours, and solar entrepreneurship—from financial whizzes and software engineers to creative marketers and, most importantly, passionate consumers.

For decades to come, the massive makeover of our inefficient, stored-solar-power (aka fossil fuels) conversion grid to a future-state direct solar, sunshine mesh needs to be designed, financed, built, and maintained—all of which will take time and a huge amount of work. Happily, a huge amount of work means an equally big number of new jobs in existing trades and professions as well as in innovative categories, like the "remote solar designer" position that Sungevity created: engineers who design a solar system for your home using software and aerial imagery so that they never have to bother you at your house.

Adoption of solar power is a key solution both to the economic downturn and to the climate change calamities caused by our dependence on ol' King CONG. Just as the rise of the steam engines from the mineshafts of England was a harbinger of the Industrial Revolution that swept the globe, the mass adoption of solar power will transform our economy in ways that are broadly beneficial. In the past few years, solar job creation has outpaced the greater economy tenfold. Meanwhile, the fossil-fuel electricity-generation industries shed 2 percent of their employees. There are now more than 100,000 workers in the US solar industry, which means they outnumber coal miners in this country.

We're playing in the big leagues and can't drop the ball. To win the game, we need to stay in the game—and to do that we have to build political momentum and economic vitality. Our efforts are already paying off. The conservative intergovernmental International Energy Agency (IEA) is now predicting that by 2050 most of the world's electricity could come from solar power. The keyword here is *could* because it all depends on what energy policy our nation chooses, what we as voters and consumers demand, and the kinds of solar businesses our best and brightest build over the next few decades. The IEA forecasts that we could create astounding wealth and opportunity—a many thousandfold increase in solar adoption in just 40 years. As a campaigner with Greenpeace, I spent years protesting the lack of consideration that the IEA gave to clean energy, and now the agency is even more bullish on solar than I am!

Imagine for a moment how much work we could create with 50 percent of our electricity coming from different forms and applications of solar power. The solar industry currently produces less than 1 percent of electricity and employs 100,000 individuals. Does that mean 5 million more people would soon be solar workers? Probably not, because with scale comes efficiency (meaning some of the work could be done through automated technology), but certainly many millions would be engaged in the industry. A study by the Institute for Local Self-Reliance showed that making the United States a 100 percent solar nation would create nearly 10 million jobs. So even if the solar industry were to displace every employee who makes a living working for Dirty Energy (an impossible scenario), we would still have a net gain of 7 million jobs—and we hope that there will be places in the solar industry for those who leave Dirty Energy (see chapter 5).

Some of these job gains will be in the opportunity that solar power unlocks in adjacent spaces: in building and roofing materials, in financial products banking on the sun, and in digital and software companies needed to harness this potential and adapt it to our current condition.

Why Solar Will Win

I believe that everyone is going to go solar because it's better—not just better for the pocketbook, not just better for the planet, not just better for jobs or the economy or security but because it's the best idea ever—better than the wheel and the automobile and human flight and Google.

The idea is spreading that solar power is better than fire. It provides the services we get from fire without burning stuff first. This reality is catching on and will soon be ablaze. Indeed, I believe going solar is a shift in what it means to be human. It's our next big step.

So far, evolution's great achievement was getting past eating raw food that we could "hunt and gather" and instead cooking it so that it wouldn't spoil and therefore lasted longer. Humans' lives improved by leaps and bounds with that one change. And with a cooking fire we could also warm a cave, change our habitat, and light up the night, which changed our lives for the better. And then we used our ability to light fires to boil water to make electricity. And in many ways that has made our lives better still. Fire is good. And fire in a wire, as an electric current, is even better—no local pollution, no smoke. For many billions of people, it's a blessing. Besides warming us, cooking our food, and lighting our way in the dark, electricity allows us to travel on trams and trains and planes, entertain and educate ourselves, and even connect with our friends using social media. The amazing thing about solar-panel technology is that it allows us to do all of that without boiling water first.

This book is about *change*—how that next evolutionary step will come to pass, the economic and social drivers that will make solar use commonplace, the businesses that will cause the Solar Ascent to happen, and how *you* can help bring about these changes. I've seen the worst of the "fossil-fool" economy, but I've also seen the potential of solar while starting one of the fastest-growing companies in the sector, which is the fastest-growing sector in the economy. And from all I've seen, what I know is this: We need the Solar Ascent. We need solar advocates, activists, entrepreneurs, and consumers to bring about this change. And who are the revolutionaries who will lead the charge toward sustainability, health, and prosperity? In one big powerful honest word: *us.*

Let's do this!

What You Can Do as a Rooftop Revolutionary

▶ Experience firsthand how you can benefit from the power of the sun. Get a solar quote (www.sungevity.com) for your home and encourage others to do the same.

▶ Check out the annual American Solar Energy Society's National Solar Tour (www.nationalsolartour.org) to see homes just like yours, powered by the sun.

CHAPTER 2

Empires of the Sun

Dirty Energy's Petty Politics

> The fossil-fuel industry and its allies in Congress clearly
> see the solar and wind industries as a threat and will try
> to kill these industries as they have for the preceding
> two generations. They want this to be a five-year
> aberrational period.
>
> —CONGRESSMAN ED MARKEY, *WIRED*
> MAGAZINE, JANUARY 2012

PICTURE ME IN APRIL 2010, JUST OVER A YEAR AFTER BARACK
Obama's inauguration. I'm at the White House representing
Sungevity at a lavish Earth Day reception, where environmental
champions, such as solar pioneer Denis Hayes, are being cel-
ebrated. (Oh, how grand this all is: the manicured Rose Garden
in bloom, the bow-tied servers, the slender flutes of champagne,
the tasty hors d'oeuvres—real treats for all us overworked and
underdressed activists and entrepreneurs.) After the ceremony,
I and Rhone Resch, the head of the Solar Energy Industries
Association, move with the dazzled throng across the lawn
toward the president. As I approach, I'm not exactly sure what
I'm going say to him. But when face to face with the leader of
the free world, I deliver the message that's been on my mind

since long before his election: "Mr. President, you should put solar panels back on the White House."

Obama doesn't skip a beat. He nods firmly. "Good idea, Let's do that," he says before being swallowed up by the wave of well-wishers.

Let's do that.

His response rings in my ears, and I recover from the brief connection over a stiff drink with some solar-industry friends at the bar on the South Lawn. Some of them had heard the executive imprimatur I'd just received, and we all agree that the time is ripe for us to urge the president to reinstate solar on the first family's home.

Thus we kicked into high gear what we would call the "Globama Campaign." Our team at Sungevity had already sent First Lady Michelle Obama an interactive quote, using our proprietary satellite and aerial-imaging software to design and engineer a solar system for the White House roof. To promote the plan, Brian Somers had created a website (www.solaron thewhitehouse.com), but after the president's statement at the Earth Day reception, we were prepared to make a more public call to put solar back on the world's best-known residence.

As we said in the letter to Mrs. Obama, "We need a bold statement from the first family, saying that clean energy works, saves money, creates jobs, and is something that 'I want for my home.'" In particular, we wanted to shine a light on the economic benefits of going solar—the jobs and the savings on energy costs in the household budget, even if it is an unusual home—and to see the power of the office used to make these benefits plain to people across America.

Will Obama make good on the "Let's do that" proclamation he gave me and every solar advocate within earshot? We're hoping he will, but we're not holding our breath; instead we're taking steps to ensure that he does. (You can help; see "What You Can Do as a Rooftop Revolutionary" at the end of this chapter.)

A Political Football

Why do we in the clean-energy field have to doubt the intentions of our elected leaders, who should already know how our nation would benefit if we were to make a real commitment to widespread use of solar power? We've been relentlessly beating them over the head with facts and figures—the massive job creation that solar adoption would bring about, the significant savings on our energy bills, the huge reduction in pollution, and ultimately the increased independence from foreign oil as we move our mobility to electric vehicles. And why has there been so much resistance from many of our leaders in taking solid next steps? The answer, in short, is politics.

Perhaps this is best shown in a potted tour of the United States' flirtations with a real solar-energy strategy. Let's start with the energy crisis of the 1970s, when Jimmy Carter was in office, just 15 years after photovoltaic cells were invented. Back then our conflict with the Organization of the Petroleum Exporting Countries (OPEC) caused a shortage of gas and an alarming surge in gas prices. Carter led a campaign for energy conservation and efficiency—bundled up in his sweater while encouraging America to turn down the thermostat—and held up a fist as he declared that the energy struggle was "the moral equivalent of war." In today's energy struggle, we hear an eerie echo of his concerns as we risk actual war due to the continued crisis of our oil dependency in the Straits of Hormuz, our supply line of Middle Eastern oil. To combat fuel shortages and their

devastating costs to the public, Carter created the Department
of Energy and a national energy policy, which was quite positive, including direction on price control and development of
new technologies, especially wind and solar power.

Perhaps one of the most innovative moments in his presidency was when he had solar panels installed on the White
House to heat water for the building. In the speech to mark
the occasion, he talked about the fork in the road that America
had reached on its energy journey, and he imagined what the
panels would someday say about this era in the nation's history.
The technology could end up "a curiosity, a museum piece, an
example of a road not taken," he said, "or it could be just a small
part of one of the greatest and most exciting adventures ever
undertaken by the American people—harnessing the power
of the sun."

Sure enough, those solar hot-water modules were taken
down during the next presidency, Ronald Reagan's, despite the
fact that they were working perfectly, providing 1,000 square
meters of solar-collecting surface that saved the White House
$1,000 per year on its energy bill. When one of Reagan's people
was asked why, the spokesperson responded that solar panels
were "not a technology befitting a superpower." Apparently,
acceptable superpower technology to Reagan meant lifting
the ban on commercial processing of nuclear fuel—thus wid-
ening the playing field for nuclear power, despite the Three
Mile Island disaster that had just occurred—and attempting
to open Alaska's Arctic National Wildlife Refuge to oil drilling.
But straight, efficient, and sustainable sunlight? *Nah,* believed
Reagan and his people—*that stuff's for wimps.*

This is just one example of how solar has become a political football. Partisan politics has attempted to muddle the real

benefits of solar energy for America and for all people. When an incoming administration belonging to one political party deems an energy technology unsuitable for the stature of the nation just a few years after the previous president, who was of another political party, pronounced the technology a sign of the future, we can guess we're headed into a negative spiral of silly rhetoric and irrationality. But get this: the administration of George W. Bush—a staunch Republican, like his hero Reagan—put solar *back* on the White House. He had the National Parks people, who run the place, install the panels on a maintenance shed behind the building to power the White House grounds and the swimming pool's hot tub, but they had to do it while the president was out of town lest he be seen as reversing the Reagan-era doctrine against solar on the grounds.

Americans against American Innovation

As many commentators have noted over the years, issues around energy policy have been caught up in America's culture wars, and the rise of solar energy has been the casualty. Conformity to the view that climate science is bunk, clean energy is ineffective, and coal is the only way to make electricity is enforced by intense social pressure. Right now, as *Grist* writer Dave Roberts put it, "Republicans who stray, who say anything accommodating, who even acknowledge that scientists might be on to something are savaged by the base and the conservative media complex."

Sometimes this pressure spills over to contain the modest aspirations of liberals. Let's look at President Obama and his response to the fate of the solar panels that Carter (a fellow Democrat) had installed on the White House and which Reagan took down. Just recently, a team of Swiss filmmakers found the modules while researching the history of Carter's energy policy. In the great 2010 documentary *A Road Not Taken,* the film crew takes the modules to the Smithsonian Institute and then down to the Carter Center in Atlanta, where the modules are indeed accepted as museum curios—fulfilling Carter's prophecy. Bill McKibben, the famous climate activist and founder of the group 350.org, took one of them to the White House in 2010 in support of the Globama campaign, to demand that they be reinstalled. His request was rejected.

The common sense that should prevail around clean energy is falling prey to America's maddening politics. Why do you think so many influential media figures have changed their tune on energy policy? Look at Newt Gingrich, who in 2008 went from endorsing Al Gore's view of climate change to adopting a "Drill, baby, drill; dig, baby, dig" line through his nonprofit American Solutions for Winning the Future. He took $825,000 from the coal giant Peabody Energy Corporation and $500,000 from Devon Energy, an oil and gas player.

The corrupting influence of money in politics is clear, but the good news is that average Americans from both parties understand this. Not a lot of Libertarian and Tea Party types in Iowa voted for Gingrich during his 2012 presidential bid, and it was because of this kind of "serial hypocrisy," as Ron Paul put it. As I've said time and again, and I'm going to keep saying it: we need to urge our politicians to stop taking money from energy companies and their lobbies so that they can make honest decisions about where our power should come from.

In an ideal world, the choices we make about our electricity future should not be influenced by our political affiliations. Clean energy is neither Republican nor Democratic—it's good for everyone. It's not red or blue. (I personally like to think of it as orange, the true color of the sun.) It shouldn't be right or left, but right up front. We have to rise above petty and partisan agendas.

Nasty politics from various quarters opposed to the success of clean energy and solar power doesn't come solely from one group or another. Take, for example, labor union members who traditionally vote Democrat but may be more likely to oppose prosolar policies than those who belong to the ultraconservative Tea Party. While some union members realize there's more work to be had in a distributed energy solution, many still count their livelihood on well-paying jobs in power stations. On the other hand, many conservative Americans look forward to the Solar Ascent because they know that the jobs it creates in the community—in sales, installation, maintenance, and a myriad of other areas—won't be offshored and will be readily available to them. This creates true independence and gives us the liberty we deserve.

Yet, currently, the Republican Party composes the bulk of advocates for the fossil-fuel industry. This mostly comes from the professional political hacks around the party. Take, for example, Grover Norquist, lobbyist, conservative activist, and one of the strongest opponents of clean energy, who has focused his bullying sights on the Renewable Portfolio Standard (RPS), one of the most effective positive energy policies in the United States. To Norquist the RPS is the new, skinny, but increasingly popular kid in town, and Norquist seriously wants to crush him before he grows up into a federal clean-energy standard or RPS equivalent being considered by Congress.

In an op-ed on the politically influential blog *Politico.com,* Norquist and a colleague regurgitated some oft-made claims of the fossil-fuel lobby: that clean-energy requirements in some states were costing jobs and money, that legislators would be wise to repeal laws that require some amount of clean energy in their electricity system to level the playing field (as though pitting nascent clean-energy technologies against the behemoths of the fossil-fuel industry would be a fair match), and that subsidies for the renewable-power industry are a waste. In the games surrounding energy policy, the latter is one of the greatest fudges of all—the idea that fossil-fuel businesses don't receive subsidies while the clean-energy businesses do. We'll dive into the details of the many and varied subsidies we provide for all manner of energy systems later, but for now suffice it to say that *everybody* in the industry gets some and King CONG gets the most.

In a rational conversation, we would be looking perhaps at a cost/benefit analysis and trying to calculate the value of solar energy versus, for example, coal-fired power to determine whether legislators should support mandates for renewable energy. Fortunately, many of our legislators have not listened to the likes of Norquist and are able to determine the facts for themselves, which show the benefits of clean energy, especially solar.

For example, in Colorado the RPS requirements to meet 20 percent of electricity needs by 2020 will be achieved eight years in advance, that is, in 2012, and will save customers $100 million in electricity costs while creating thousands of jobs and substantial tax benefits. On the other side of the ledger, coal costs more than it creates in value, according to a 2011 study in the *American Economic Review,* which estimates that in the United States coal creates roughly $53 billion in damages per year—a cost that is more than twice as high as the market price of the electricity. The estimate does not include "external effects such as those that take place through water, soils, noise, and other media" or carbon dioxide and its effect on climate. When the authors added in estimates of the cost of carbon dioxide pollution, they found the gross estimated damages caused by power plants to be more than 30 percent higher.

The bottom line is that putting partisan politics before American competitiveness in clean energy will cost more American jobs and lives in the years to come. That's the real problem with all this politicization around Solyndra's downfall. Americans are pioneers, which entails taking some risks. We make great entrepreneurs, and we should not delimit the arenas we work in to exclude the fastest-growing industry in the world. Investing in the energy technology that will power the world is a good risk to take (all entrepreneurs in every new field take these risks), but do note: in Solyndra's case, its loan-guarantee program was set by the Bush administration, so the investment in the company (and by extension the industry) wasn't an Obama or liberal interest, as some in the media would have you believe. Overall the clean-energy loan-guarantee program has had a higher than 90 percent success rate. That's something of which both parties should be proud and should be doing more.

The Madness Goes Global

All the world's a stage, and this political farce around energy has been playing out for decades. I've personally had many supporting roles in this theater. In 1992, for example, I was at the United Nations (UN) meeting in New York where, after much deliberation and many months of late-night sessions, world leaders drafted the United Nations Framework Convention on Climate Change, a global effort to slow global warming. But young attendees, including yours truly (I was there as a journalist and a youth activist), began to smell a rat in the framework when George H. W. Bush sent a message to the UN that "the American way of life was not up for negotiation"— meaning that Americans were neither going to stop using fossil fuels to create electricity nor give up driving their SUVs.

To protest Bush's statement and the abdication of responsibility by other world leaders, some of us printed posters and stuck them on the toilet doors of the UN building on First Avenue. The signs read: "Bathrooms closed—toilets flooded due to global warming; contact US delegation for more information." We were hauled over the coals (pun intended) for this act by then–Undersecretary General Maurice Strong, but we pointed out that this is what young people do when they're not heard by their elders (and supposedly betters): we resort to daubing slogans on toilet walls in protest.

I'm all for a clever, well-intended wall scrawl, but now that I'm older I realize that it's much too easy to use these methods to rail against our wishy-washy leaders and ineffective legislatures. Doing so is fun and effective in its own way, but I wonder now whether we could get real solutions from this kind of action at the UN. Getting behind an encouraging example of political leadership could. Take the former president of the Maldives, Mohamed Nasheed, who could very well have become the mouse that roared in this energy debate. Certainly, if deeds and not words counted toward volume, Nasheed would be the most-heard leader in the international negotiations.

The Republic of Maldives is an amazing country of fewer than a half million citizens. It's set in the middle of the Indian Ocean and comprises about 100 populated islands and many hundreds more that are unpopulated, some of which have become resorts. Most islands are less than 1 meter above sea level, which means they're highly vulnerable to sea-level rise caused by climate change. This and other factors, such as extreme weather and changing ocean currents—which in turn have affected the country's fisheries—are causing Maldivians to worry about their future.

An Encouraging Example of Leadership

Nasheed, who served as the fourth president of the Maldives from 2008 to 2012, was the first democratically elected president of this small Muslim nation in several decades. (He was forced to resign in February 2012, in a coup d'état.) His predecessor was a ruthless dictator who had had Nasheed tortured and placed in solitary confinement for being an activist and a dissident journalist. When Nasheed became what he calls the "accidental president" following a political campaign that was given great momentum by the 2004 Indian Ocean tsunami, he set about facing the biggest threat to his country: climate change.

Nasheed famously brought attention to the cause by holding an underwater cabinet meeting near a coral reef (probably one of the most photographed government events in the country), in which he and his ministerial colleagues wore SCUBA gear while signing documents with waterproof ink against the backdrop of a coral reef. He championed climate protection at the international conferences on the subject during his presidency. Not a lot came of his efforts to broker a deal at the UN Copenhagen Summit in late 2009, except for a documentary film on the subject titled *The Island President* and some money to build sea walls in the Maldives against the rising tide. So perhaps his greatest effort to respond to the climate crisis was to make the Maldives the first carbon-neutral country on Earth.

Toward this end Nasheed jumped at the offer we at Sungevity made, in conjunction with our friends at 350.org, to put a solar electric solution on the presidential palace, a beautiful colonial building built by the British in downtown Malé, the capital of the Maldives and home to about one-third of its population. Most of these people probably pass the palace every day on their way to work or school or the beach; it's on a small island of 150,000 people, and the Muliaage, as it's known in the local language, is right in the middle of the city. As such it was the ideal place for the president to kick off his efforts to take his country solar.

I was fortunate enough to fly there in October 2010 and work with a couple of colleagues on the installation of the 11.5-kilowatt solar system, which consisted of 48 solar panels—which the president himself helped us install—and would cover the electricity load of more than two average American homes. They would offset 195 tons of carbon and save the Maldives $300,000 in electricity cost over the life of the system. We spent about a week on the roof and in the attic of this magnificent old building, wiring the first solar electricity into the nation's grid with the help of some of the palace's maintenance team. We had an opening ceremony, of course, which the president attended, as did most of the media on the island. We also held a telephone news conference, for which only a few of the many members of the international media we'd invited dialed in.

And therein lies the rub: Here you had an articulate and charismatic world leader, a Nelson Mandela for his country, and a Muslim president of a democracy that went through a revolutionary uprising five years before the famous Arab Spring of 2011, and yet there was almost no interest in his efforts to address climate change or create a solar economy. It seems that politics dictates that this is a nonstory for most of the media. Yet President Nasheed carried on. A little more than a year later, he was back on a roof, personally installing a solar system on the administrative buildings of his government just down the street from the palace. And, more importantly, he negotiated funding with the World Bank to create a program that would install wind and solar power to displace most of the diesel-based electricity in the country.

Now despite being deposed, Nasheed is continuing the work and agitating for fresh elections, and his efforts will be key to his country's survival. As in many island economies, right now almost all the electricity in the Maldives is derived from burning diesel in huge generators housed in shipping containers. This causes horrendous air pollution and exorbitant costs per kilowatt-hour. As discussed earlier, solar succeeds best where the true cost of fossil-fuel-based electricity is accounted for, and on an island such as Malé that is a truly heavy burden on the community. The numbers are astounding: one-quarter of import expenditures are on diesel fuel, and the Maldives utilities are literally running out of land on which to place the containers that house the diesel generators.

Moreover, this model of fossil-fuel import dependency is entirely untenable from a national security point of view and as an economic proposition going forward. If the price of oil were to exceed $100 per barrel for an extended period of time, the country would go bankrupt. Then the oil industry would no longer deliver the fuel by ship, and the country would be left without electricity. This scenario is already playing out in other island communities: it's the curse of dependence on fossil-fuel electricity. So the president's push to get solar energy adopted across the country makes sense; indeed, it makes dollars and sense.

Lessons Learned from the Maldives Microcosm

This story about a small country somewhere on the other side of the planet and its courageous leader is really a cautionary tale for us all. It makes sense to adopt solar energy broadly, but the market can't dictate rational results; instead it's a function of political economy, with a heavy emphasis on the word *political*. That is, markets don't exist in a vacuum, and in the United States the pressure to maintain dependence on fossil fuels is foisted on us by politicians and interests of many stripes, ranging from big utilities like San Diego Gas & Electric to labor unions like the International Brotherhood of Electrical Workers. In California there was a proposition in the 2010 election to undo the greenhouse-gas laws, known as Assembly Bill 32, a ballot initiative paid for by Texas oil companies and a few others, such as International Coal Group Inc. The bad news is that this kind of attempt to peddle influence and subvert democratic processes in order to protect ol' King CONG is commonplace.

The good news is that people rarely fall for it—and in the Golden State 65 percent of voters rejected the Texas oil companies' Dirty Energy proposition.

In another example of Dirty Energy foisting continued fossil dependence on a community and the community fighting back, just a year earlier the utility PG&E spent $50 million on a campaign to stop a local clean-energy initiative in Marin County. The proponents of the initiative—called Community Choice Aggregation—had only a few hundred thousand dollars (a slingshot to the utility's bazooka) to fight PG&E's proposition, yet the clean-energy group (and California residents) won by a clear majority against the energy giant.

Polling consistently shows that normal people across America like this idea: clean power of the people, by the people, for the people. Again, it doesn't matter what side of the political aisle you stand on or support or what religion you believe in (or even whether you're a religious person). A lot of people are realizing that solar power works and that it's better than what we've got. What makes it better may be different for different folks— for some it means energy security and reduction in dependence on fossil fuels, while for others it means a reduction of pollution and the slowing of global warming, and for others still it brings the satisfaction of generating electricity on their own roof and not at the end of some long wire.

"Local clean energy" is an idea that appeals to people across the political spectrum. In October 2011 a poll from the University of Texas at Austin showed that out of more than 3,400 consumers surveyed, 84 percent were worried about US consumption of oil from foreign sources and 76 percent about a lack of progress in finding better ways to use energy efficiently and develop renewable sources. Politicians who don't heed these numbers should be held accountable, for they've failed to create what the people want: prosperity and sustainability. Our elected officials are obligated to act on an energy plan that can bring us both. We must hold our leaders' feet to the fire of solar power. Let's all take a pledge to stand with the sun and demand that *all* candidates in *all* races take it with us. Let's take it global and call for *all* representatives in *all* countries to resist the partisan and chauvinistic politics that are contaminating our energy choices.

A decade ago, when I was working for Greenpeace USA around the California energy crisis—a result of that state's dependence on Texas gas companies like Enron—we supported a ballot initiative to issue bonds for solar and wind installations by the San Francisco Public Utilities Commission. We were astounded that 73 percent of the electorate voted yes to solar—a result I'd never seen, and I started working on my first election in 1983, when I was 12. Three quarters of a US community agreed to raise $100 million to spend on something!

Solar shines through the smoggy sameness of politics as usual and speaks to people. We must demand that our elected officials tell us how they'll support solar if they have the privilege to represent us, what positive energy policies they'll pursue to stop our dependence on foreign and fossil fuels, and what their plans are for job creation in the clean-energy industry.

We have to raise our voices in chorus. We have to say to all the politicians we elect, from our nation's president down to our neighborhood's councilmember or supervisor, "Repeat after me: we want clean, local, affordable energy, and we want it now." And then we must make sure that these leaders stay true to their word.

What You Can Do as a Rooftop Revolutionary

▶ Know where your politicians stand on energy and vote for those who support (or at least take an open-minded approach to) renewable energy.

▶ Go to www.facebook.com/solaronthewhitehouse and click "Like" to get behind the momentum to put solar back on the first family's home.

▶ Separate oil and state. Visit www.priceofoil.org to help end King CONG's tremendous influence on our government.

▶ If you're a business owner (large or small), join the ranks of Apple, Nike, and thousands of other businesses across the country to pressure the US Chamber of Commerce to change its stance on climate change. Visit www.chamber.350.org and join the movement.

▶ Sign the Solar Bill of Rights—www.solarbillofrights.us—a statement that provides a clear policy foundation we can use as we move to a cleaner and more secure energy future.

▶ Urge your elected officials—local, state, and national—to sign the Solar Pledge (www.rooftoprevolutionbook.com/solarpledge). The Solar Pledge calls on anyone who represents us in elected office to commit their support to solar market development and to oppose policies unfairly supporting fossil fuels.

CHAPTER 3

Role Models for the Rooftop Revolution

> The secret of life is to have a task, something you
> devote your entire life to, something you bring
> everything to, every minute of the day for the rest of
> your life. And the most important thing is, it must be
> something you cannot possibly do.
>
> —HENRY MOORE

THE WORLD ENERGY COUNCIL 17TH CONGRESS, IN HOUSTON, Texas, 1998: We were on a mission. Our first goal was to highlight the evils that Big Oil wrought on frontier areas like the Amazon; the second was to let all the international bigwigs attending what was until then the largest gathering of petroleum giants that the days of easy oil were over.

Just after 3 a.m. on September 16, 1998, five of us crouched down at a section of the fence that protected what was to become Enron Field, just opposite the George R. Brown Convention Center, where all the official meetings were being held. We rolled under the fence while two others kept an eye out for the roaming security guards who took turns patrolling the perimeter. My backpack, with the stuffed koala I'd had since I was a kid sewn into a side pocket, hardly fit through the hole because it was so jammed with ropes, harnesses, and other climbing gear. We worked quickly, our bodies humming with adrenaline. Once on the other side, we raced toward the enormous idle crane in the middle of the field, mud sucking at our boots. When we reached the crane's ladder, we ascended it in the order we'd planned—I went last because one of my tasks was to install a steering-wheel lock on the hatch at the first landing, to slow down anybody who tried to catch us. This precaution proved unnecessary, as nobody pursued us, at least not then. By the time the sun rose with a lambent glow over the Houston skyline, we had tied our anchors, rappelled into place, and unfurled what was then the biggest banner (more than 1,500 square feet!) ever used in an American act of civil disobedience:

HOUSTON, WE HAVE A PROBLEM.
STOP NEW OIL EXPLORATION.

The attendees of the World Energy Congress were there to make deals, and the oil companies were there to strike new finance arrangements and negotiate concessions with governments to open up some of the new fields then becoming "hot," like West Africa and parts of Latin America. It was an infamous, rare gathering of oil executives, pipeline proponents, and coal chiefs to plot with politicians and bureaucrats of various kinds. Our organization, Project Underground, and the Rainforest Action Network were there to release *Drilling to the Ends of the Earth,* a report we'd been working on for a year, on the ecological, social, and climate imperative for ending new petroleum exploration.

"The energy industry needs to supply energy—not oil," one of my colleagues said in the report's news release. "If oil companies invested serious capital in developing sustainable alternatives to fossil fuels, the quality of life on this planet would increase for everyone."

My friend Oronto Douglas was in town. He'd been a lawyer for the great, nonviolent Nigerian organizer Ken Saro-Wiwa, whose cause of ending oil exploitation in his native Ogoni land I'd supported as an activist in Australia. In 1995 Ken was tried for a murder he couldn't have committed and was convicted in a Nigerian kangaroo court and then executed—all at the behest of Big Oil by his country's dictatorship, an act for which the country was suspended from the Commonwealth.

Oronto had watched while Ken was hanged. Ken's family sued Shell for ordering his death, and in 2009 Shell settled out of court for $15 million. So for us in Houston, trying to tell the world the terrible things that happen in the places our oil comes from, Oronto was a first-person witness to the calamities brought to indigenous people around the world at the cutting edge of oil and gas industry development.

The whole country has been affected by the wars for control of oil in the Niger Delta, even though the people there have been polluted and poisoned by it since it was first discovered by Shell in the 1950s. To this day Oronto struggles with the consequences of oil in his homeland and seeks justice for the victims. He's now a special adviser to the democratically elected president, Goodluck Jonathan.

Back then in Houston, Oronto endorsed what we said to the media, with firsthand knowledge of the resource curse Nigeria and many other places suffer because of oil. Our statements back then—and I think that they stand today—came down to this: when the climate is in danger of global meltdown, and when irreplaceable natural areas are being destroyed, and the indigenous people who live there are being displaced, it makes absolutely no sense to continue exploring for more oil. The carbon logic was clear: burning the coal, oil, and gas reserves we already knew we had in 1998 would risk runaway climate change. Looking for more petroleum, and spending precious time and money on the pursuit, was a waste, and we wanted the world to know.

Our efforts had the desired effect. We got the attention of thousands of commuters on the Eastex Freeway as they wound into the city; we drew media choppers and reporters, along with their cameras; and we raised the ire of the sheiks, energy ministers, and oil executives exiting their limos on their way into the conference. We swung gloriously in the wind like a big spinnaker crew on the front of a yacht. We even felt heroic as we were taken to the ground by big ladder trucks from the fire department, and we were almost exhilarated as we were dragged off to the police station.

It was a triumphant day! That is, until we hit the county jail and were told we were being charged with multiple felonies—such as the serious offense of conspiracy to commit property damage—instead of the misdemeanor trespassing charge we'd expected. Apparently, an energy exec or someone equally high up had persuaded the burghers of Houston to take a "Don't Mess with Texas (or Big Oil)" stance against us, and if the charges stuck, we'd be in jail for years, if not decades. Our bond was 10 times that of a typical alleged murderer's, and I was held for three days in a cell with 22 other inmates, some of them drug runners from Colombia who actually befriended me, sympathizing with our campaign to stop frontier oil development in places like Nigeria and the Amazon.

With gratitude and relief, we accepted the offer of legal counsel from a bulldog of a lawyer named Mike DeGeurin—the

"Johnnie Cochran of Texas"—who obtained for us massive media exposure on a national scale and even interest from the likes of *Court TV* and Oprah Winfrey. Ironically, the more our persecutors came after us, the more our plight interested the media, which clamored to hear our side of the story.

My favorite moment was doing a news conference while still locked up—still dressed in the jail's orange jumpsuit, my hands cuffed and ankles shackled. I was taken to a briefing room, where we got to justify our stance and blast Big Oil and Dirty Energy at the same time. Local TV broadcast the appearance live, so I was greeted by cheers when I arrived back at my cell. These guys inside and many more outside got to hear the reasons for our protest, and most of them agreed with our side. Realizing this, the city dropped the most serious charges against us. We pleaded guilty to a misdemeanor and were released.

While I sat waiting with my fellow jailbirds for all of that to transpire, two of our colleagues from Greenpeace were back at the convention center, using other methods to change minds. These friends—Iain MacGill (who became a prominent academic promoting clean energy in Australia) and Gary Cook (who went on to force Facebook to unfriend coal in a great 2011 campaign)—were pushing DVDs on any conference delegate who would take them, hoping that the package would inspire a change of heart in these energy-industry diehards. The video package contained plans on how British Petroleum (now BP), one of the world's largest and most dastardly oil corporations, could become the world's most profitable energy company by scaling solar manufacturing and making it affordable enough to displace conventional electricity.

On hearing about these friends' efforts, I was facing a fork in the road, and knew I'd need to choose. Was it better to risk life and limb swinging off cranes and getting arrested, or was it more effective to go inside the system? If we really wanted to force accountability and action, was the best path through continued acts of protest, or was it through the equally subversive, but less felonious, approach of trying to make friends with our adversaries? Protest without solution can be quixotic and weak, but solutions without some sense of justice in their design can actually perpetuate problems. Simple technical fixes just aren't sufficient to redress the power imbalances in our society. I pretty quickly decided that both approaches are necessary and can be powerful in their own way, but at the end of the day I realized that whichever tack we might choose, our energy and attitude must remain positive.

Raising an Army of Solarrikins

As I remember the events of 1998, I keep thinking of the Australian concept of the *larrikin*. Look it up and you'll see that the word is usually used to describe an unsavory sort of hoodlum, scoundrel, or ne'er-do-well. But as the son of Aussies, I know there's much more to it than that. Larrikinism has come to evoke a tradition of irreverence, a disregard for propriety, and a willingness to challenge authority—all done with a pinch of self-deprecating humor and charm and a certain positive energy too, which is one of the main traits of the larrikin, I believe. People who dare to challenge the status quo should embrace these qualities—whether swinging from heavy machinery or journeying into a lion's den of teeth-baring oil bosses, armed only with some DVDs to try to get the word across that there's a better way to boil water. We need to be courageous, irreverent, forward-thinking, and—most of all—positive.

To revolutionize our energy system for the good of our country and the world, we need leaders in the solar-energy movement to be firebrands and troublemakers, passionate activists and savvy, scrappy entrepreneurs. We need them to be solar larrikins—indeed, *solarrikins!*

I've always believed that if you want to change the world, you must first realize that the world *can* be changed—or, to state it in a more positive way, you have to know that *you* can change the world. I've found that truly great activists and entrepreneurs share this knowledge. These people have also been willing to rock the boat, allow themselves to obsess about their passions and goals, and fight their way out of the muck they're sure to find themselves in from time to time, whether we're talking about a team of college students set on creating the next big Internet sensation like MoveOn.org or YouTube, or the couple working toward their dream of opening their small town's first farm-to-table restaurant as a part of the movement for community-supported agriculture.

Yet those who want to grow the business of solar face a unique challenge. These entrepreneurs have ol' King CONG to contend with, and they need a particular determination and sense of humor to take on such a behemoth. We can't be scared off by the aggressive methods the fossil-fuel industry used to kill off earlier generations of the electric car and a lot of electric public transportation systems to protect their interests. But the solarrikin grits his teeth, braces for the fight, blows a raspberry, and keeps in mind that the struggle is half the fun, no matter how bloody the battle.

As Dan Epstein, who runs a business incubation and acceleration organization known as the Unreasonable Institute, says, entrepreneurs have to be "unreasonable" in the sense that

George Bernard Shaw meant when he said, "Progress depends on the unreasonable man." Unreasonable men and women are going to be the activist-entrepreneurs who lead the charge away from Dirty Energy companies that cling to the unsustainable stored power of King CONG and toward the direct solar resources that we get free from the sky. These are the folks who will get sustainable, affordable, transformative solar products into the market on a worthwhile scale.

But where are all these rooftop revolutionaries, these role models, these activists and entrepreneurs who are going to act as the examples of what I call the New Greatest Generation— the folks who are going to stand up to the challenge of our time, bring on the best form of electricity generation, and create a universe of opportunity that makes the Internet look like small beer? Well, they're all around the globe. Allow me to introduce you to some who have inspired me and are sure to inspire you. Look 'em up, read their stuff, replicate their approach to business and life, emulate their attitudes, and begin the work of transforming energy in our world. We need them, but more importantly we need *you* to look upward, not underground, for electricity.

Mohamed Nasheed: Carrying the Torch

You've already met Mohamed Nasheed, who epitomizes the kind of solar champion we need. If reelected he plans to create a demonstration project of our global solar potential. The personal challenges that this man has taken on are hard to overstate. Aside from having suffered exile and torture, he now carries the torch for the fledgling democracy of the Maldives, whose economy hinges on how much it must spend on oil imports for electricity and how much money it can generate from tourism.

Nasheed's plan was profound. His government was collaborating with resort owners to bring renewable energy to the country—not just to tourist locations but also to the islands neighboring the resorts, where the typical Maldivians live. There were efforts afoot for a premium tariff to support solar-energy deployment and solar-electrification pilot projects funded by the World Bank and brokered by the Maldives' government.

In the Energy Experts blog at NationalJournal.com, Nasheed explained to an American audience why he put solar on the palace: "This is a beginning step on the road to making the Maldives completely carbon-neutral by 2020." He continued with a question and a challenge: "What can the United States do to make similar progress to transition away from dirty, increasingly expensive fossil fuels and toward wind, solar, energy efficiency, and other clean, renewable technologies?"

You're most likely not the activist ex-president of an island nation, but like Nasheed you can be a "mouse that roared" in the energy fight (novelist Leonard Wibberley's description of a small leader who dares take on a behemoth). You too can speak the truth about the power in the world and challenge your representatives with the same kind of question Nasheed asked: What can *you* do?

Jeremy Leggett: Making the Case for Business

When I was in the Maldives in October 2010 to install the solar system on the presidential palace, we were invited to accompany Nasheed to a seminar on sustainability, on a resort island called Soneva Fushi, which is one of the nicest places I've ever visited. Your hosts take your shoes from you when your seaplane lands, so you immediately feel the soft sand against your feet when you reach the island. (You get your shoes back when you leave.)

Sadly, this little strip of paradise is being threatened by climate change. The coral reef around it is "bleaching"—showing the slow death of the tiny organisms that build the reef, due to the slowly rising water temperature—and extreme weather events have eroded some of its foreshore.

While on Soneva Fushi, I reconnected with one of my other solar heroes, Jeremy Leggett, a phenomenal activist and entrepreneur. He was my first boss at Greenpeace in the early 1990s and in many ways served as a role model for me. He should be a role model for the whole world as well.

Jeremy is now the chairman of a company called Solarcentury, one of Europe's largest solar developers. Before beginning Solarcentury, Jeremy was the chief scientist for Greenpeace International and one of the key influencers of the Kyoto Protocol, an international agreement under the UN Framework Convention on Climate Change that bound 37 countries to reduce greenhouse-gas emissions. He's written several fine books on the subject of climate change and carbon-based energy systems. Before he joined Greenpeace, he was a professor at the Royal College of Mines in London while working for the petroleum industry on the side. Now he's set on building big business to forge the solar economy.

Jeremy opened my eyes to the value of "campaigning corporations"—businesses fighting for social change. His book *The Empty Tank: Oil, Gas, Hot Air, and the Coming Global Financial Catastrophe,* does a great job of explaining the future technology choice we face between "solarization" and "coal-ification." He's tireless and ever willing to try something new to bring on the Solar Ascent. His life's work and passion have shown that businesses can join the fight against Dirty Energy.

In 2011, alongside Friends of the Earth, Jeremy got his company to sue the UK government all the way to the High Court of England for cutting the financial support for small solar systems it had set up only a year before. These companies established that the Tory government had failed in its public process to consult with affected parties before making the policy change. This was a small but important victory because the main risk to solar companies now is uncertainty, and on-again, off-again policies like this undermine investor confidence.

Back in the Maldives in 2010, through our long-term lens as climate activists, Jeremy and I checked in on the state of play in solar globally, and we concluded that we needed more—and we needed it yesterday. At a bar on a reef during a glorious sunset, we reveled in the seemingly impossible but ultimately inevitable rise of solar. We discussed how some of the low-hanging fruit, especially the business opportunity to displace diesel grids on islands like the ones we were enjoying, were the bite-sized victories on the march to the Solar Ascent. We determined to help make that happen by encouraging other entrepreneurs to fill that niche, and we returned to the work in the United Kingdom and the United States.

So, all you fledgling solar entrepreneurs out there searching for a hero to show you how to gain success and channel your passions into your business—Jeremy is your man. His vision of using solar panels as the skin of every building and combining them with smart microgrids, even in places like those quaint, cloudy islands in the United Kingdom, should inspire nation builders everywhere. It's an awesome opportunity, though the challenge is building the business to do it. Who of you out there is up for that challenge?

Tom Steyer: Fighting the Good Fight

I got back to the States just in time for the final throes of the campaign to reject California's Prop 23 on the November 2010 ballot. This proposition, as mentioned earlier, intended to trick voters into overthrowing California's legislation regarding climate change mitigation known as Assembly Bill 32. This AB 32 is the overarching law on the subject in California, which is one of the world's top 10 economies, and the legislation contains a broad sweep of efforts to reduce carbon emissions. It includes targets for pollution reduction and a market-based mechanism supposedly to raise funds for a clean-energy transition. A couple of Texas oil companies, Valero and Tesoro, and a number of other fossil-fuel industry players had placed the proposition on the ballot in an effort to prevent regulations that they thought would be harmful to their businesses. Prop 23 asked voters to delay implementation of AB 32 by popular vote. This was a classic example of Dirty Energy beating up on the clean-energy industry and public health to protect its own interests.

The oil companies' lead antagonist was an investor named Tom Steyer. He's a man who has made it. He runs a hedge fund called Farallon and was tapped by some as a potential candidate for treasury secretary when Obama was elected in 2008 (yet he wears the same tartan tie every day and drives a 1990s Honda Civic). A tireless advocate for clean energy and the advanced-energy economy, Tom co-chaired the No on 23 campaign with George Shultz—the former secretary of state under Reagan—to crush the proposition. In this unlikely but dynamic duo, we had a couple of out-of-the-box solar champions signing up for the fight to save our economy.

It's important for the world to know that the folks fighting the good fight range from hedge fund managers to Republican secretaries of state and that the fight surrounding solar energy is what binds a lot of us together. In this campaign California venture capitalists, Republican governor Arnold Schwarzenegger, and community organizations representing people of color (who wanted to stop the erection of polluting gas-fired power plants in their neighborhoods) up and down the state joined forces under Steyer and Schultz's leadership to defeat the dirty-oil proposition by convincing the electorate that what's good for the planet is good for jobs.

The victory against Prop 23 may go down in history as the moment when the populist support was proven. Certainly the jobs-versus-environment debate was almost put to bed. The rate of growth in clean-energy businesses since 1995 is 10 times more than the state's average job growth rate. People know this intuitively. Nearly two-thirds of the population voted against the proposition. The victory party in San Francisco saw some strange bedfellows fist-bumping, backslapping, and celebrating the rise of clean energy despite the best efforts of some of King CONG's handmaidens to stymie it.

Another significant takeaway from the Prop 23 defeat of which Tom and all the grassroots activists who fought it should be proud is that it demonstrated the electoral power of the clean-energy cause. No political analyst worth his or her stripes could miss the signal that the defeat of Prop 23 sent: clean energy had crossed over to become a mainstream movement with broad support from a vast majority of voters. How many other big issues do diehard Republicans and diehard Democrats agree on these days? Moreover, the No on 23 campaign shows that these issues can draw out the big guns from across the political spectrum to fund a well-organized ass-whooping, which is what they gave the other side. As I wrote on a blog with one of my venture-capitalist friends, "The genie is out of the bottle."

It may be premature to say that the jobs-versus-environment debate has been won, but the uplifting reality that burst onto center stage in the election of 2010 was that job growth through clean energy will be an important issue in future elections and that green-job growth is a proven fact (as discussed in chapter 5)—and facts are stubborn things. Renewables attract more bright, young talent moving from other careers than does the Internet or any other sector. The solar industry now employs more than 25,000 Californians. As we scale our percentage of the electricity supply from 1 percent to maybe 20 percent, there will be a lot more jobs coming from the Solar Ascent. Here's hoping that our tartan-tie-wearing Tom will continue to carry the movement forward.

Danielle Merfeld: Advocating as an Intrapreneur

Some rooftop revolutionaries will build their businesses as entirely new enterprises in the service of bringing solar to the fore. Others will be *intrapreneurs*—those who work within existing institutions or companies to drive the Solar Ascent. An inspiration on this front is Danielle Merfeld, a young, spirited mother of three from Upstate New York. Danielle leads General Electric's solar business unit and has dramatically risen through the ranks of GE, a giant 100-year-old corporation—not an easy task for a female electrical engineer working in a male-dominated field.

Passion and brains are the trademarks of her craft, which she has used to help GE see the ways it can integrate solar into much of the rest of the grid it helped build. A mind-blowing 25 percent of electricity comes through a GE device, whether the transformer on your block or the bulb in your bedroom—an astonishing fact that shows that this heir to the legacy of Thomas Edison is very much a part of the firmament. Danielle is helping move this grandpa of a company into the twenty-first century.

GE's solar division is set to boom, just as its wind business has been its most profitable over the past decade. The company's ability to integrate solar panels with storage solutions, inverters, and transformers and all sorts of technologies critical to the infrastructure of the existing grid will create a huge amount of value. *Forbes* reported that the first major market that GE's brand-new solar division is going to step into will be solar farms around wind turbines, which the company is also going to build and finance. More than 1 million solar panels will be produced in a US factory each year, and they're going to go to GE's own wind farms and will probably connect to the grid through devices that the company made. It's a beautiful business model of vertical integration that could result in a massive opportunity to create clean electricity.

Danielle's internal advocacy has likely inspired her colleagues to see the light and start this business, while other big companies are still clinging to the past. That is a critical role that many people reading this book could fulfill: opening the eyes of their bosses and others to see how they can take part in the Solar Ascent.

Sven Teske: Spreading the Sunshine

Sven Teske is German friend of mine and another of my superheroes because he has long helped everyday people understand their own superpower, which is their ability to go solar. Sven's also an engineer by training and has one of the most brilliant minds imaginable, but he's also one of the sweetest, most affable people you'll ever meet. (For those of you who think pairing the ideas *German engineer* with *sweet* and *affable* makes as much sense as mixing boiled potatoes with ice cream, think again. Most of the German engineers I've met truly are.) He's tall and curly haired and can speak multiple languages, which he does with aplomb as he travels the world spreading the good news about solar electricity uptake.

Sven is also one of the least-heralded champions of the solar industry, which is odd because he not only directed Greenpeace's renewable-energy efforts internationally for more than a decade but also helped start a solar-energy cooperative in Germany that currently has 100,000 customers. He has heavily contributed to the International Energy Agency's *World Energy Outlook* (*WEO*), an important status report published annually for the energy industry. I remember when he joined me in Australia to participate in the release of a solar-generation forecast and he ran a half-marathon just for fun the day after a grueling 24-hour flight. He pops up in the most surprising places, Yellowstone National Park for example—hiking with his family by day and editing *World Energy Outlook* reports by night.

In the nineties and naughties, Sven was a one-man publishing house. He generated reports for a full-scale model for renewable-energy uptake, solar-thermal technology adoption, and concentrated solar-industry developments for specific regions around the globe. These reports mainly addressed solar generation and were often dismissed by critics from the mainstream electricity sector. Sven consistently and meticulously demonstrated the accuracy of his forecasts over several years, however, actually underestimating the uptake of renewable-energy technology, and therefore demonstrated that these industries were exceeding the expectations of even Greenpeace. In this way he's earned great credibility. Whereas a decade ago he was rejected by the International Energy Agency and the United Nations, he's now listed as either author of or contributor to many of their studies because he has so persistently proved his authority and pressed the case for clean energy.

Sven shows the optimism and the enthusiasm of a true rooftop revolutionary, and his refusal to listen to naysayers makes him unstoppable and inspiring. Adopt that frame and the sun shall reign! He's an example to budding solar enthusiasts that they too can promote the power of the sun for everyone and spawn businesses that serve it up. Sven is now in the midst of doctoral studies, and I can't wait to see what brave new world he conjures next. Sven is the kind of guy who inspires me to ask myself, *What the hell am I going to do to bring on the sun?*

Alex Voigt: Saying Farewell to Fossils

Alex Voigt is an entrepreneur and another larger-than-life German friend of mine who has reached great heights in the service of the solar economy. He has founded several solar companies, such as Solon, a large module manufacturer. Some of these ventures grew to $1 billion or more in market value at the height of the German market and have since gone bust and then been reborn by being bought out of bankruptcy. You know you've been in the solar industry for a long time when you've been through the full life cycle of a corporation! Alex's work ethic, combined with a sense of fun (you're as likely to find him watching performances of the Ukulele Orchestra of

Great Britain as you are to see him sitting in a boardroom with a bunch of suits) to get through tough times as a businessman, make him a role model for entrepreneurs everywhere.

His latest venture, a company called Younicos, seeks to displace diesel-generated electricity with solar and clean-energy storage systems. In many settings, we still use diesel generator sets to produce electricity, for example on islands where getting other fossil fuels is difficult. Hawaii gets more than 90 percent of its electricity from the burning of this oil product, which is why its electricity is extraordinarily expensive by US standards. Most Hawaiians pay more than $0.30 per kilowatt-hour, which is twice as much as many folks pay on the mainland. As one way to scale solar and storage technology for a clean economy, Alex and his friends at Younicos are using island markets as a target for their business.

Alex's work is incredibly timely because, as the price of oil hovers around $100 per barrel, the likelihood that these islands will be able to afford to import diesel fuel for even a few more years, let alone the rest of the century, is dangerously small. This point was made clearly in late 2011, when Tokelau and Tuvalu, two small countries in the Pacific Ocean, were left without water because they had no rain for more than six months; they had to fly in diesel fuel to run generators to power desalination systems so people didn't die of thirst. If anything underscores the critical stage we're at, it's the fact that their lack of rainfall was a result of climate change and their only recourse was to burn more fossil fuels for very expensive electricity to get water.

Alex and his team have created a testing environment that's capable of demonstrating the true potential of clean energy for island economies. The test bay, as they call it, is a warehouse on the outskirts of Berlin, inside of which they can simulate in real time both the weather on an island and the electricity usage by its population. As part of the feasibility analysis for a renewable-energy microgrid to be built on an island, Alex's team runs a "dress rehearsal" of the wind- and solar-energy inputs through the scale model of an island's electricity system. It also monitors the inhabitants' ability to meet the load or demand for electricity in various situations. For example, if a tree on the island falls and takes down a power cable, the disruption to the transmission grid will be reflected in the test exercise in Berlin as the team seeks to maintain uptime there with renewable-energy inputs. This incredible capability has been used to pitch utilities that service islands such as Graziosa in the Azores, where the utilities can implement a power-purchase agreement with Younicos to provide the island's electricity supply.

Alex's vision of displacing diesel-based electric supply on some island with a solar solution, combining battery storage and energy efficiency, should inspire you. It's an economic no-brainer, though the challenge here is financing the projects on all the islands that should switch out diesel for juice straight from the sun.

Alisa Gravitz: Partnering for a Green America

Someone else who saw the light early in this journey is Alisa Gravitz, who went to Washington, DC, in the 1970s during the Carter administration to work on the promise of solar energy, which was just starting to be realized. Like many in that era, she probably experienced somewhat of a false start in a career building the sunshine-based grid that we know now is possible. She stuck with it, however, forging a fantastic nonprofit in the 1990s known then as Co-Op America and now called Green America.

In 2001 I worked with Alisa on a series of reports on solar potential throughout the United States, in particular California, through the research and advisory firm Clean Edge, while I was director of the Clean Energy Now campaign at Greenpeace USA. Alisa has continued her collaboration with solar companies as well as her advocacy, most recently with Sungevity.org, which we set up in early 2011. This is a group marketing effort that spreads our solar lease product while supporting groups that champion the solar economy. We pay them with our marketing-allocation budget for referrals if they help their constituents go solar, and this effort has raised $400,000 for Alisa's organization and other nonprofits.

Green America members who go solar host parties to tell their friends and neighbors how cool it is. We pay Green America if any of those partygoers join the Rooftop Revolution. Like good organizers, Alisa and her base are also building power for the next big collective action, which is to pass legislation for Clean Energy Victory Bonds. So at the house parties they also talk about this proud American tradition that could be applied to the fight against Dirty Energy. This is a great example of how starting people on the road to the Solar Ascent can also engage them in the ongoing work that needs to be done.

Billy Parrish and Dan Rosen: Crowdfunding Solar

Another exciting Sungevity partner is a company called Solar Mosaic, which we helped incubate in 2011. It was founded by a couple of characters, entrepreneurs Billy Parrish and Dan Rosen, who may well revolutionize not just the rooftop but the very way we make money and save for our retirement. The company is called Solar Mosaic because it's a platform for crowdfunding of solar projects. You can go to www.solarmosaic.com

and for $25 buy a solar "tile" in a project you like—one investor might want to buy a tile for a local church, for example, while another might choose her tile on a sports center. Over the life of that solar system, your money is repaid and then some; in other words, you own a share in a productive asset on a roof somewhere and make a good return on the investment. And when I say "good return" I mean it because the value of the return generated by a solar system is around 6 percent—certainly better than the 1 or 2 percent that you might earn with a CD or similar investment instrument.

What sparked this pair to build this brilliant business was a common cause: antipathy to coal-fired power, which they got to know firsthand working as energy activists on the Navajo reservation in Arizona. For those who don't know the history, the Navajo Nation has been the site of some of the largest strip-mining operations ever seen, mostly at the direction of Peabody Energy Corporation. And most of the coal was burned either in the Mohave generating station in Laughlin, Nevada, or at the Navajo generating station near Page, Arizona, which in turn shipped the electricity via transmission cables to Los Angeles, Phoenix, or Las Vegas, some thousands of miles away. Strip mining in Navajo country left it a mess, with the land seriously degraded and water sources fouled.

As if this weren't crazy enough—to be burning coal to boil water to generate steam to drive a turbine to create electricity to sell thousands of miles away—the way the coal got from the mine to one of the power plants was an abomination: the power company created what it called a "slurry," which means it powdered the coal close to the mine, mixed it with water, and then pumped it through a tube to Nevada, where it would be dried out and burned. This depleted the water supply. Water in

Arizona is somewhat of a scarce commodity, and on the Navajo Nation it's sacred. Through a spirited campaign over many years, the community was able to stop this madness and dismantle the Mohave Power Station in Laughlin. (You can even watch the implosion of the smokestack on YouTube.) Billy and Dan were living on the reservation at the time and were inspired by the struggle to start Solar Mosaic.

Perhaps the sweetest twist to this tale is that Billy married a woman named Wahleah Johns, one of the project managers from Black Mesa Water Coalition, the nonprofit working to shut down the Navajo power plant. Wahleah and her colleagues are now trying to build a major solar project on the site of the old mine. This would be a multi-gigawatt development, and because it's already close to transmission lines on degraded land, it may be the best use of the site. It could be paid for with a Solar Mosaic. Because the company is in startup mode, Billy and Dan have decided to walk before they run and are providing solar home solutions for residences on the Navajo reservation, whose people are among the poorest in the United States, with an average annual income of less than $10,000. More than 18,000 people there don't have running water or electricity.

This must be one of the vilest ironies in American life. These poor but proud people have had more than $100 billion worth of coal extracted from their lands and have had high-voltage transmission cables running over their heads for decades, yet the system of electricity generation that we've all had to suffer has been unable to service them with this basic commodity. Solar systems on their homes are clearly a superior solution.

Billy and Dan demonstrate that feisty campaigners can make good, by bringing their values to the world of finance. This is the moment in history when major new economic models will be built on the convergence of new energy and information technologies. With a crowdfunding platform on the web to back solar projects, Solar Mosaic is showing the way. Ingenuity—the unique combination of things—is a key to our solar success.

Zhengrong Shi: Epitomizing the Can-Do Approach

While Billy and Dan are feisty and successful campaigners, some who represent the best and brightest in the New Greatest Generation may not actually consider themselves such. Zhengrong Shi, PhD, is known to many as "the Sun King." He's a Chinese-Australian national who earned his doctorate in photovoltaic engineering at the University of New South Wales in Sydney. Then, back in China, he received a grant from the local government of the city of Wuxi, in Yixing Province, to build a factory to produce solar cells and panels for export, and in the past decade he has built it into probably the largest solar company in the world. Next year his company expects to produce 3 gigawatts of solar modules, which is the equivalent of building three nuclear power plants in a year. More than 10 percent of that will be deployed in China, which is very good news for reducing coal burning. His creation is really taking the fight to King CONG!

Yet when I visited China a few years ago, Dr. Shi gave me some personal time, remembering when he and I were on a panel together in Australia's old Parliament House—I at Greenpeace, he at a solar startup in China called Suntech Power. I saw in this behavior the kind of rebel baron (rather than robber baron) that I believe makes solar entrepreneurs unique. There will be many big businesses and fortunes built in coming years on the back of the Solar Ascent. I hope to see in the people who lead these companies some of the traits that Dr. Shi brings: a keen sense of can-do business and a commitment to helping the world. Almost like Robin Hood meets the Goliath-defeating David.

Julia Mason: Inspiring Authorities to Adopt Solar

You don't have to be an electrical engineer, have earned an MBA, or even have struck out on your own to be a solar superstar. I recently discovered the story of a young woman named Julia Mason, a student at Monte Vista High School in San Ramon Valley, California—the home of Chevron—who inspired her entire school district to install 3.3 megawatts of solar in the next couple of years. Like many in California, the school district is working to save money through solar-energy adoption—$2.5 billion to date—so it can afford more teachers, computers, and books. Julia was critical in making this happen by demonstrating several traits of a great solar entrepreneur: commitment, patience, and a lot of heart. She and her classmates were able to persuade the school board that not only could they "afford to go solar" but they "could not afford *not* to go solar."

Eden Full: Using Low-Tech Tools to Track the Sun

Another incredible case in point is the wonderfully named Eden Full, a young woman you can Google and see present a TED talk on YouTube. As a high-school student working on a project to enter into a science fair, Eden came up with a low-cost tracking solution to increase the productivity of solar systems that could be implemented in developing countries. Her solution increased the output of a given solar system by about 40 percent, which would make it worthwhile for many more people to buy a solar system.

Eden's idea is to create a tracking solution to put on solar panels that can track the sun using local materials that don't cost much. In a truly ingenious model, she used bamboo and water to accurately track the course of the sun through the sky, day in and day out, for less than $40. Now she's trying to build a business that can deliver this simple but elegant solution to people around the globe, and at the tender age of 20 she has received the backing of some of Silicon Valley's most famous investors.

Peter Theil, one of the founders of PayPal, picked Eden for a fellowship that he funds to preempt kids like her from going to business school. Instead he supports entrepreneurs who create value and invent things, just as humans always have without the benefit of two years of schooling and hundreds of thousands of dollars in debt—an idea that makes a lot of sense. He has suggested that there's been a failure in our era to invent things of true value; instead we've become satisfied with new apps and simple entertainment improvements. You can argue with the view, but certainly in regard to infrastructure there's some truth to it. Theil believes that serious innovation has stagnated and that talented technologists should be concentrating on meaningful engineering, the way our predecessors focused on crossing oceans and continents and rocketing to the moon.

We were promised jet packs, though the current crop of high-profile startup "innovators" are rehashing old technologies rather than changing the way we live in the world for the greater good. As wrong as they may have been, the pioneers of the oil age, and the advocates of the steam engine before them, *thought* they were bettering the human condition; and now we really do have a technology and a resource in solar power that can truly improve our lives. It's for this reason that we need rooftop revolutionaries—solar entrepreneurs and solar activists. The good news is that there are many among us now like Eden Full; the bad news is that we need many more.

Mobilizing the New Greatest Generation

Clearly we need more diversity in this effort. We need more women involved and more work done at the bottom of the pyramid, to provide electricity services for the hundreds of millions of people who still can't take it for granted. A company called Simpa Networks in India is adapting the solar lease model from the United States and applying it to small solar solutions for families across the subcontinent.

At Sungevity we support a program called Every Child Has a Light, which is donating solar charging solutions to Zambia so the country can develop its education system. This ability to tap their household superpower—to create electricity when and where it is most needed—can improve the lives of millions of people and can change the course of a nation. At one level they are replacing toxic kerosene—an oil byproduct—in people's houses but at another they are providing the opportunity to learn to read and write and to join the modern world without dependency on something that causes pollution and death and that costs money.

The flow of opportunity it unleashes is like the flow of electrons on a solar panel, building from a trickle in one kid's life into a torrent of value creation. The big breaks from the Solar Ascent will be downstream. As in information technology, the jobs were not simply in making motherboards or modems but rather in the creativity that was opened up by the power of the personal computer and the productivity gains created with the advent of networked computing. So too will solar power unleash many opportunities beyond the nuts and bolts of building solar systems. If we can foster the ingenuity required to maximize our solar potential—especially in developing countries, where electricity is needed most—there will be enormous benefits, especially jobs. I have a vision for 2020 that we can create 1 million businesses worldwide at an average valuation of $1 million each, and, as Sramana Mitra points out in her 1M/1M blog (www .sramanamitra.com), which is devoted to supporting entrepreneurs to bootstrap themselves, this momentum could create $1 trillion in value and 10 million jobs.

The 1 million entrepreneurs who will start these 1 million businesses will need the traits of the people introduced in this chapter. What do they all have in common? Clearly, they come from all walks of life—from heads of state to C-level execs to students—but they all have grit, determination, courage, and imagination as well as an ability to partner with others and combine forces creatively.

Maybe the one big difference that separates the solar leader from leaders in other fields is that solar activists sometimes have to take an entrepreneurial role and that solar entrepreneurs have to be activists. One must be a little bit of the other to spread the power of the sun to everyone.

What You Can Do as a Rooftop Revolutionary

▶ Become a role model yourself: get involved, spread the word, get a solar quote, go solar, and save our economy *and* our environment!

▶ Support Green America's call for Clean Energy Victory Bonds at www.cleanenergyvictorybonds.org.

▶ Become a solar billboard: get a watch or a Kindle cover or a bag or something that uses direct solar power to demonstrate how cool this stuff is!

CHAPTER 4

Take a Walk on the Sunny Side

> I'd put my money on the sun and solar energy. What a
> source of power! I hope we don't have to wait until oil
> and coal run out before we tackle that.
>
> —THOMAS EDISON, IN CONVERSATION WITH
> HENRY FORD AND HARVEY FIRESTONE, 1931

SOLAR *SCHMOLAR*, SAYS OL' KING CONG—JUST LEAVE WELL enough alone: Pay a small fee when you move into a new home, and we're ready to serve. Just flip a switch, twist a knob, or press a button, and—*voilà*—your beer is cold, your shower is hot, and your TV casts its warm glow onto your grateful faces. We'll take care of your energy needs and your energy future. (Just make sure you get your monthly check into the mail.) Why change? Why even consider that solar mumbo jumbo? It's impractical, unreliable, unviable, inefficient, unaffordable, and overly subsidized. Plus those solar panels on your roofs would be downright ugly. Maybe there's something to solar power in the distant future, but if it's really such a great energy alternative, why hasn't it caught on in the 50 years or so since the technology was first developed? In any case, don't worry your pretty little heads about that now—we're looking into it, and we'll get back to you. Someday.

This is what the coal, oil, nuke, and gas industries want you to believe, and they've embarked on a massive and consistent campaign to instigate fear, uncertainty, and doubt to make their case against solar energy.

Sometimes their message is subtle—for instance, when Dirty Energy proponents call solar an "alternative" energy (in the way a brutish older sibling dismisses the little brother he wants everybody to ignore). Or when they call it "cute"—as Microsoft's Bill Gates said when attempting to start a nuclear renaissance. Or when they call it a "future" or "emerging" technology, which is often Chevron's approach. In all these descriptions, "Don't bother with solar" is the clear subtext.

Sometimes King CONG is more blunt, such as the Koch brothers' "Solyndra = Failure" campaign ads and when Exxon-Mobil CEO Lee Raymond appeared on PBS's *Charlie Rose* show and simply stated, "Solar is not a viable replacement" for oil. Then he went into some complicated claim about how you'd have to cover all of New Jersey with solar panels to produce the energy Exxon gas stations contain. "Do the math," the oil titan challenged. I found myself jumping up and yelling at the screen. It's completely feasible to cover an area the size of New Jersey with solar panels! There's a lot of roof space—plus parking lots, road sidings, and degraded land—in the United States, and it adds up to a lot more than the area of the Garden State. New Jersey is actually quite small, and with only that space we could replace the energy supply of a company that holds the biggest share of the gas market. The truth is, a 1,000-square-mile area of solar panels would provide all of our country's electricity needs, which is less than 10 percent of the land used by the oil and gas industry today.

And then there are the outrageously sneaky lengths that CONG's soldiers will go to get into our heads. Take haughty Lord Christopher Monckton—the British politician and climate change denialist—who was caught on tape encouraging members of the Australian mining industry to create a Fox News–style media network and use it to further the mining agenda.

It's amazing how much fear, uncertainty, and doubt (FUD) these people throw around to make some of it stick—and to fool the world into thinking that clean energy isn't ready for prime time. The best example of this is how Solyndra has been portrayed in the media: When you compare the onslaught of coverage (fed by CONG's PR people) surrounding the solar company's default on its $500 million government loan with the relatively minuscule coverage of the revelation that US taxpayers had lost between $31 billion and $60 billion to waste and fraud by military contractors during the wars in Iraq and Afghanistan, you know you're up FUD creek.

The congressionally commissioned report that exposed this outrageous waste of taxpayer money was released the same week Solyndra shut down operations. It prompted 11 news articles and less than an hour of television coverage between August 28 and September 23, 2011, even though the reported cost to taxpayers was at least 56 times greater than that of the Solyndra failure. In the time between August 31 (the date Solyndra suspended operations) and September 23, six major print outlets discussed the collapse in 89 news and opinion items. Television networks discussed Solyndra for more than 10 hours—eight of which occurred on Fox News alone. (That's a ratio of 10 to 1 on TV and almost 2 to 1 in print!) The media-watchdog group

Media Matters, which documented this disparity in coverage, reminded its readers that Congress had planned for some failures with the Department of Energy loan guarantee program (which was actually set up before President Obama's time) because it was a portfolio of risky investments they were making to help launch some new energy companies, and they had set aside $2.4 billion for the cost of defaults. Of more than 40 clean-energy companies that benefited from these loans, Solyndra is the only project that has failed by the spring of 2012.

King CONG is just plain *wrong on solar.* Solar adoption *is* practical, reliable, viable, efficient, and affordable. And I'm going to tell you what CONG doesn't want you to know.

The Adoption Curve

First let's tackle the misconception (which CONG wants to drill into you, so to speak) that solar power isn't viable because it's been around for 50 years and has yet to be fully embraced. The truth is, solar energy has caught on at a faster rate than most other energy sources did. Other game-changing technologies have taken at least that long to be understood for their true potential.

The steam engine, for instance, took more than a hundred years to be recognized as the incredible resource that it is. Around 1690 the steam engine was used underground to pump water out of mines—ironically, coal shafts in northern England that were below the water table. After five decades people realized its value and put it to work aboveground driving pistons for machinery in mills.

And then, a decade or more later, a clever chap named James Watt put it on wheels to create a locomotive that was first used to haul coal out of mine shafts. (It's from this use that we derive the word *horsepower* because, ever the creative marketer, Watt was looking for a way to explain the potential of this engine, and he did so by relating it to the amount of coal that a mule could drag out of a mine per hour.)

It wasn't until 1884 that an engineer by the name of Charles Parsons used his new steam-turbine engine to drive an electrical generator.

A similar tale could be told of the automobile, which, while invented in the late nineteenth century, was not widely adopted as a form of transportation until after World War II. As for the automobile's fuel system, it wasn't until 1964 that petroleum became the major source of fuel in the United States—despite the first commercial oil well having been drilled in the 1850s and all those fortunes made in the early 1900s.

History is accelerating in terms of how quickly technology can be commercialized, but given the mind-blowing nature of solar we shouldn't be surprised that it's taking some time for solar panels to become the dominant form of electricity generation on the planet.

If solar power takes as long as petroleum (or oil) did, from discovery as a system of energy use to majority share of its market, it could be dominant by the 2020s. We're right on track for that, but we'll likely get there sooner due to economic and environmental imperatives for clean energy. King CONG's suppression of solar power's adoption goes against the tide of history. And CONG has been so shrill in its opposition to common sense and good economics that it seems to be driven by greed—and by the fear that the rise of a new, competitive industry is going to affect its bottom line.

Which brings us back to those things you've heard—about why solar isn't ready to provide your house's power. The fossil-fuel industry makes a lot of money for its various executives and shareholders—and making money is fine unless it comes at the expense of others. It's clear that this is increasingly the case. These interests want everyone to believe that there's no real option, as this is how they can maintain their wealth and power. The motivation is plain, as greed and fear of losing privilege have long driven people to do things not necessarily in the interest of the greater good. At the very least we should take their views with a grain of salt.

The Myth of Inefficiency

I hate to repeat myself, but how efficient is the steam-based energy system, where you take sunlight that was stored 200 million years ago in some form of plant material, dig it up from where it was buried, truck it somewhere, burn it to boil some water, use the steam pressure to drive a turbine that will lose much of the energy as heat, and then transmit the electricity generated to some point of use many miles away?

With solar energy you take that solar power directly captured by panels, at the point of use, and—presto!—use it as electricity. Just the first step of the process by which we extract stored solar energy from fossil fuels in the steam-based system is less efficient than the photovoltaic effect, which we use in solar systems. Photosynthesis, which was the process by which plants took up the sun's energy in chemical bonds, works less efficiently than the 15 percent conversion of photons to electrons of the standard solar module. Then there's a step down in efficiency across every one of the other stages of the steam-based system as a source of electricity.

When comparing these two systems, which would you agree is the more efficient?

Another commonly held misconception that prevents people from investing in solar panels is that they'll become much more efficient in time, so you shouldn't buy now. It's true that solar panels will become increasingly more efficient, but this does not negate the fact that a solar panel is the superior way to get electricity right now.

But hold on, CONG pipes up. What's the rush? Wait until solar panels produce electricity at 20 percent efficiency in terms of photons to electrons; or wait five years, for 30 percent efficiency; or wait a decade, for 50 percent efficiency. This ignores the fact that at 15 percent efficient conversion of photons to electrons, solar panels make electricity both cleaner and more cost-effective. If we had waited for a car to be as efficient as a solar panel is right now, we'd still be driving around in horse-drawn buggies.

The Future of Solar Power

Some of the cleverer solar antagonists are framing solar energy as a "future technology." You may have seen ads about fossil-fuel companies "investing in solar for tomorrow" to make themselves out as good guys, concerned about the environment but unable to yet use solar power. This was a lot of the content of BP's Beyond Petroleum marketing campaign, even though it spent a factor of 10 times as much on new oil and gas development than on solar in the decade it ran the ads. And in 2011 it shuttered solar operations altogether.

In other words many fossil-fuel interests are peddling the message that they care, but in truth they're procrastinating. This "not yet" message cracks me up because they know as well as I do that space travel and satellite technology are all solar powered and have been pretty much since we first went into space.

Solar is not a future technology but a technology that's ready for us now—the people here on Earth who are concerned about bills and our energy future.

Subsidies

Ah, subsidies: King CONG's favorite fight. And why? Because CONG wants you to believe renewable energy is being overly subsidized. Yet *all* energy is subsidized, especially the fossil-fuel industry. It is currently estimated that here in the United States oil companies are receiving $7,610 per minute in tax breaks— that's $4 billion per year. And fossil-fuel subsidies are perverse, while renewable-energy subsidies are broadly working. It's true that there can be problems when politicians pick favorites, like Solyndra, but the most egregious problems are the now-permanent and accepted subsidies provided to the fossil-fuel industry.

The US government's $50 billion-plus-per-year outlay for conventional energy sources distorts the US energy sector by subsidizing mature companies whose business models and core technologies work well, are insanely profitable, and in many ways dominate markets that are neither highly volatile nor even competitive. The other way our government supports them is to continue to turn a blind eye to their externalities, or true costs— whether that's maintaining a military presence in the Middle East (to secure our access to oil) or tolerating the intense impact of conventional energy on human health and ecosystems. We have already mentioned the threat to humans in terms of air quality effects and climate change, but conventional energy also degrades our environment, which has an immediate economic cost in terms of diminished resources (such as water). All of these costs should be added in when we tally up the corporate welfare we give these companies.

You can quibble over numbers, but fossil-fuel subsidies far outweigh those for renewable energy. The Environmental Law Institute reckons that the US government gave more than $70 billion worth of subsidies to fossil-fuel companies between 2002 and 2008. In that time about $2 billion went to the solar industry. US Congressman Earl Blumenauer calculates that the government is committed to spending more than $40 billion to subsidize the fossil-fuel industry from 2011 to 2015, while no more than $10 billion is scheduled to flow into renewable-energy businesses.

The federal government has a long history of investing public dollars in energy via tax credits, subsidies, and other incentives. The agency that tracks such things, the US Energy Information Administration, found that in 2007 subsidies to nuclear were 9.6 times higher than those for solar; natural gas and petroleum subsidies were 11.2 times higher; and coal subsidies were 22.2 times higher. Some people think that this has changed a lot recently due to "Obama-era stimulus spending," but the American Recovery and Reinvestment Act made only small advances toward equal treatment of the technology. Even in 2010 coal subsidies were still 20 percent higher, nuclear subsidies were 120 percent higher, and natural gas and petroleum were 148 percent higher than solar subsides. More importantly, 93 percent of the fossil-fuel and nuclear subsidies were permanent, whereas almost 70 percent of the solar subsidies were temporary stimulus-bill subsidies, which reduce the certainty that the clean-energy industry needs to attract investors.

A better way to think about these subsidies is in an apples-to-apples comparison of the early phase of each technology's adoption. Just the first 15 years of investment in each energy sector reveals tremendous discrepancies: $1.8 billion per year (in inflation-adjusted dollars) was spent on subsidies for oil and gas industries in their early days compared with just $400 million for all renewables, including wind and solar. And today, a hundred years later, tens of billions are still spent supporting oil companies each year, even though they've clearly established their businesses.

The problem is that, over time, fossil-fuel subsidies have been *increasing* per unit of energy or jobs created rather than declining as the industry matures. Remember that solar energy creates between three and seven times as many jobs as fossil fuels. As mentioned, many of the fossil-fuel subsidies have also become permanent, such as the tax credits granted to American gas- and oil-drilling industries, which use the money to finance their wildcat and fracking forays; this reduces their innovation drive.

And all the while, the companies behind these efforts have been increasingly profitable: ExxonMobil was the most profitable corporation in history for much of the 2000s. So it's receiving government money while making exorbitant profit. And since the mid-2000s it's been shedding jobs; indeed, Big Oil downsized its workforce by more than 10,000 in the second half of this century's first decade. In 2010 alone the top five oil companies reduced their global workforce by a combined 4,400 employees while making a combined $73 billion in profits—this includes BP, which that year had the infamous spill in the Gulf of Mexico. The coal industry is similarly retrenching its workforce, with the greatest losses soon to come in the Appalachians. So don't be fooled: King CONG is a part of the problem, destroying American jobs while making gobs of money and disproportionate billions in subsidies.

Renewable-energy subsidies, while smaller, have been declining per unit over time relative to the amount of power they produce. For example, in California, the major market for the Rooftop Revolution so far in the States, rebates have fallen from more than $2 per watt of solar power installed to less than $0.50 in most utility territories. So for the solar industry, we can say that government support programs have been doing their job in terms of creating an incentive for the industry to mature, increasing competition, and decreasing prices. Indeed just in the past couple of years, as the price of oil soared to more than $100 per barrel, prices for the solar consumer have fallen by more than 50 percent.

At the same time, solar businesses have boomed, and we've created jobs almost 10 times faster than the national average. Between August 2010 and August 2011, the number of people employed in the US solar industry grew 6.7 percent, to more than 100,000, which is more workers than are employed in the coal-mining industry. We explore the jobs benefits of the Rooftop Revolution in greater detail in chapter 5, but for now note the difference with the fossil-fuel industry; that is, that solar has had a diminishing subsidy over time while its prices have dropped and its employment has grown.

At the end of the day, it's dubious that renewable-market support payments should even be compared with the corporate welfare that fossil fuels have received. As the IEA writes,

> Only a small proportion should be considered subsidies or, rather, learning investments required to bring solar technologies to competitiveness. Their success would provide broad access to an inexhaustible source of energy and help give more

than a billion people around the world greater opportunity and economic freedom. By contrast, fossil-fuel subsidies only serve to perpetuate a system that is ultimately not sustainable and distributes energy production and its benefits by chance.

Reliability

"Unreliable" is a claim made by dinosaur technology when challenged by a superior new competitor. "Don't get a cell phone," the telephony industry once said, "because you may not be able to use it to call 9-1-1. Keep a landline just in case, for when you really must have an incoming phone number for your business because that cell phone toy is really not adequate to ensure service." Sure, you couldn't compare the reliability of the cell phone then to what it is now, but the benefits "that toy" provided were still life-changing. And now there are more cell phones than land lines in the world, and they work just great. Perhaps the killer factoid is that there are 500 million people who don't have electricity but do have cell phones, mostly in Africa. Cell phones have overtaken land-line use in less than a decade and are way better at providing the service of telecommunications to more people at less cost than the incumbent technology. Watch out for solar!

Actually, in one of those great "the truth is not what you expected at all" realities, solar-panel penetration into the grid *improves* reliability. This has been well modeled in New York State, where energy regulators worked out that 5,000 megawatts of solar panels spread around the state would relieve some of the stress on the grid during times of peak demand—for example, in midsummer when air-conditioners are turned up full throttle and the state's requirement can approach 34,000 megawatts, causing frequent brownouts. Lots of solar-power sources scattered around the grid could relieve local demand and reduce bottlenecks that occur when power can't move across long distances on the grid quickly enough. When you think about it as a portfolio approach to maintaining uptime or service, it makes sense that this works better than a system limited to a few large plants—it's a bit like cloud versus mainframe computing.

Reliability issues will be resolved; just as AT&T puts up more cell towers, there are ways we can evolve the grid to accept solar power. There are technical issues around plugging in to solar because, of course, the sun doesn't shine half the time, but we can make up for that by using energy storage systems, batteries, and other clean-energy generators. This is not easy stuff, but it's not beyond us. Ours is the country that created the Internet—with bidirectional, multiple input information flows cleverly organized to deliver an answer to your every question in mere seconds. We got this electricity thing!

One of the key changes in relation to reliability is the principle of "flexible and inflexible generation" and how this might replace the concept of base-load energy. For now, when we're at a tiny percentage of supply, the grid itself serves as the battery for solar power. When the sun goes down, a flexible generating resource can be turned on by the utility to match the load while the solar electricity in the system declines. Electric vehicles, for example, could have the power in their batteries drawn down while parked to meet load in the early evening. This can be technically managed now with up to 50 percent solar-panel penetration, which cannot happen for years to come in most places. After that the plan would be for solar to work with wind and demand-side management techniques—turning off loads when the demand is high—to keep the grid stable. And aside from that, if you had to, you could use a fast-ramping gas power plant to fill in any need not met by the renewable inputs.

In other words, you can have an intelligence layer that manages the various inputs and keeps the lights on, just like data centers juggle the processing power of thousands of computer servers to maintain uptime for websites and Internet service. A new range of technologies built around solar plants that store heat for after the sun goes down will add to the dynamic stability of this sunshine mesh. These colossal batteries or energy storage systems are the equivalent to the new cell towers AT&T had to put in to deal with demand and congestion in its network.

David Mills, founder of the solar-plus-storage company Ausra, has shown that by using storage you can easily correlate more than 90 percent hourly grid load and hourly solar plant performance. In other words, direct solar-thermal electricity solutions that are almost market ready can supply most of the United States' electricity needs. I bet that's why Areva—the French nuclear giant—bought Ausra (now called Areva Solar)! The IEA says that solar power with storage is expected to be available to deliver competitive electricity globally by about 2030. This means that the distinction between peak power times and baseline power usage would become less relevant, as stored solar electricity could at all times complement the fixed solar supply each day.

In summary, reliability is really a technical issue related to the grid and to scale, not something innate in solar panels. And this is going to be our challenge. The solar-panel technology works fine; day in and day out, it produces 15 percent efficient electricity from the solar power falling on it, and it's ready now. What matters is how this technology is distributed to users and how power is stored for those periods when the sun is not shining. We will have to rewire America to make this work, and energy-providing utilities will have to change their stripes—and therein lies the opportunity. While this isn't easy stuff—making a thousand points of light work together to keep the lights on—America's best have never before shrugged off something just because it was difficult. On the contrary, we embrace challenges and have been leaders in such revolutionary achievements as organizing the world's information, beating back fascists, and conquering outer space.

This is why we need the upcoming corps of entrepreneurs to be our century's New Greatest Generation. Just as electrification was the standout achievement of the twentieth century, according to *Time* magazine, clean electrification will be a significant achievement in the twenty-first century. The Rural Electrification Administration, which took America from having just 15 percent of homes being electrified in 1935 to 85 percent by 1950, is a model for how we can do it. Low-cost loan support backed by the US government spread electricity across the country (thanks, President Roosevelt!). And therein lies not just the opportunity but also the way that solar energy will become more and more affordable: scale and standardization through deployment supported by positive energy policies like the Renewable Portfolio Standard and net energy metering.

Aesthetics

My mother always told me that beauty is in the eye of the beholder, and I think that's true of the solar modules we install on our roofs. I personally find them lovely because they represent homeowners' efforts to do the right thing, save money, and achieve their higher selves by exercising their house power. But I also thought the Treo mobile phone was really lovely, and all the way through the Palm's sad saga I thought the device was just the cutest thing—so I admit that I may not be the best judge, and there may be something to some people's aesthetic concerns about home solar panels.

The truth is, people who buy them are proud of them, and the good news is there's a lot that can be done with the form factor of solar modules. Consumer feedback has already brought about changes; for example, most of our company's modules are now black-on-black because that's what the Joneses wanted. Most are also set closer to the roof so they're lower profile and appear less boxy, and some are set into the roof in a shingled design.

As with consumer electronics, there will be traps for young players working in the solar industry as companies try to roll out solar panels that are driven entirely by fashion—for fashion is fickle, as we all know. Look at the early hybrid cars, which many people felt were ugly; as the vehicles became more widespread, their appearance became much better perceived. An even more mundane example is the automatic garage door: most of them are far from things of beauty, but because they're such a common sight on most streets in America we rarely stop to think about how aesthetically pleasing they are. So it will be for solar panels.

As this is a utilitarian product, the attractiveness of the kit on the roof may become less important to many users than the service and the benefits it provides. As with the garage door, we learn to love it or at least not notice it if the control is simple and elegant. This is where we have focused our efforts at Sungevity: improving the customer experience by working on the user interface. Clever design will help address concerns about aesthetics and will buoy the Rooftop Revolution in the sea of same-same suburban houses that are not yet powered by sunshine.

Scale

The *World Energy Outlook* is an important annual report released by the International Energy Agency. I say "important" because a lot of important (and some self-important) and influential people read it and use it to inform their policymaking. Indeed, the IEA was set up during the oil crisis of the 1970s to help the world's governments preempt the supply-and-demand imbalances that led to those problems, and it has since fashioned itself as the guide for global policymaking for all forms of energy choices. The IEA is hardly a hotbed of environmentalists pushing ridiculous renewable schemes, so its *WEO* is considered key reading by Dirty Energy executives and politicians across the spectrum (although I wonder how many members of Congress have ever seen it).

In 2011, separate from the main *World Energy Outlook,* the IEA presented another study, called *Testing the Limits.* In it the IEA laid out what I consider a much more likely scenario than the business-as-usual content of the *WEO.* It looked at what would happen if the world were to make a belated but sharper change in its energy policy to get off fossil fuels by the late 2010s. The report referenced freedom from volatile oil supplies and other economic drivers as much as climate reasons for making the switch increasingly likely.

In this *Testing the Limits* scenario, the IEA found that solar energy could become the backbone of a largely renewable worldwide energy system. In this case, photovoltaics—solar-panel technology, the key ingredient of the Rooftop Revolution—will provide about 20 percent of the world's electricity generation in the second half of this century. The report projects 12,000 gigawatts of installed capacity by 2060; to give you some sense of how dramatic that vision is, currently about 50 gigawatts are installed. Solar-thermal and solar fuels will meet or exceed the capacity of solar panels by 2060, as those technologies mature in this forecast.

I know that a model is only a model and that the scenario is unlikely to play out in exactly the same way, but it's exciting to see a conservative agency projecting such a big jump in solar resources so soon. And while the model proposes fast growth (faster perhaps than one would like to even contemplate when running a business in the space), it reminds me of just how much we've surprised ourselves in the past with real, rather than projected, outcomes.

The amount of electricity that Germany generated from the sun, for example, jumped 60 percent from 2010 to 2011. The nation's solar-power systems collectively generated 18 billion kilowatt-hours of clean electricity during 2011—that's enough to power 5.1 million households. And over the past decade, forecasts similar to the IEA's—like *The Energy [R]evolution* blueprint (released by Greenpeace in conjunction with specialists from the German space agency) and *Plan B 4.0: Mobilizing to Save Civilization* (published by Lester R. Brown, founder of the Worldwatch Institute)—have underestimated the amount of electricity that the solar industry can provide.

Cost

As for the sticker shock that used to go with solar adoption, these forecasts give us new information: First, the total price for solar systems has come way down. And, second, you can now get the solar system financed, which means you "pay as you go."

Financial engineering allows you to pay for your solar panels over time instead of up front, and this is probably the most important innovation in the solar industry in the past decade.

Here's what it means for you: Forget the notion that you have to pay $30,000 to $50,000 to go solar. Now you pay nothing—nada, zero, zilch. By removing the up-front cost, we've made it easier than ever for customers to go solar; and because customers make no investment, they keep all the money that they save against their electricity cost. For example, let's take a customer of traditional utilities who comes to Sungevity. She currently pays $180 per month for her home's electricity. But once she takes advantage of our services, she pays $50 to her utility company for monthly services (because she'll need some service from the grid, at night for example) and approximately $80 to Sungevity to lease our solar equipment. She pockets $50.

This is one person's experience; 80 percent of our customers have saved on their electricity bills from day one of going solar. We now have thousands of customers in eight states. Our competitors combined have tens of thousands of customers; indeed the solar-leasing market is booming. Most solar systems installed on residential buildings in the United States are now leased or have another third-party finance arrangement known as a *power purchase agreement,* which charges them for the kilowatt-hours they use from the solar system rather than a flat monthly fee. The key is that this is the future, and most homes going solar in the coming years will benefit from some affordable, pay-as-you-go financial construct.

At the level of the overall electricity market, the IEA, in its 2011 study, adopted the position that the solar-energy industry has long held—that, as with any other energy resource, planning ahead and financing these assets makes all the difference. The example of the leasing arrangement just puts solar electricity on the same footing as coal-fired power coming out of the plug in the wall from the grid. The coal power plant at the other end of the wire was not paid for up front by you or by the company that built it. The utility company used debt and other finance capital to create that energy capacity to sell you the service of power. Now you can buy the service of solar electricity for less than the cost of dirty electricity that you get from the grid.

In acknowledging the importance of new financing mechanisms being applied to solar-power supply, the IEA observes the fundamental competitive advantage of solar, which is having free fuel over fossil fuel. It also says that other solutions fall short, while solar technologies offering "indigenous, inexhaustible resources" are actually more secure, less likely to experience price volatility once the technologies are mature, environmentally sustainable, and "the cheapest known antidote to catastrophic climate change, even if they are or appear to be higher-cost options in other ways."

So we're witnessing a sea change in how the establishment industry watchers are reporting solar's prospects, and even those "other ways" that the IEA flags as possibly costing more may not be that expensive because the up-front cost of solar is coming down so fast. The IEA notes that solar photovoltaics are already competitive with "bulk power" in many areas, particularly islands, off-grid locations, and places where solar-produced electricity is competing with oil.

When faced with these price realities, fossil-fuel execs' blood should run cold. How long can they possibly compete? What losses will they take? Big banks like HSBC, the "world's local bank," are starting to put red circles around a lot of fossil-fuel-based energy infrastructures because they may be stranded assets in the not-too-distant future. This means that their electricity production won't be able to pay for them in a sea of solar panels that generate electricity for less. HSBC analysts point to legislation in Australia and China that's likely to force fossil-fuel assets to retire early or operate below capacity. "We expect the reality of stranded assets to become more noticeable as the decade progresses," said an HSBC report. Forced closures are a scary prospect for bankers, but these will happen, and investors will get burned.

Climate Spectator's Giles Parkinson, one of my favorite business writers on this stuff, summarized HSBC's analysis of the speed at which clean energy can provide economic solutions. It notes, in particular, the impending arrival of wholesale prices for electricity from solar panels in India that are at or below the price per kilowatt-hour of coal-based electricity. This is a country that has to import hundreds of millions of metric tons of coal at prices well north of $100 per metric ton. HSBC and anyone else paying attention knows that at that price you can eliminate all subsidies for solar and it will still compete, knocking out a huge market for coal. The game is on as India ramps up its energy production: coal versus solar.

Those in the diesel-based electricity space must already be feeling that the industry's days are numbered—a bit like the people who purveyed dial-up modems when broadband came around. But so what? You may ask, How much diesel-powered electricity is there? How about almost all of Hawaii. That's right—more than 90 percent of Hawaii's electricity comes from burning oil! This is the state where the Obamas go for holidays, and 1 percent of our whole country's power comes from oil costing more than $100 per barrel! Much of this extremely expensive juice is bought by Hawaii. Worldwide there are even more easy wins to be had replacing more than 10 percent of global electricity currently coming from burning high-cost diesel fuel.

This competitiveness is why renewable electricity is growing rapidly and will continue to grow. The time is fast approaching when energy that comes from no fuel or free fuel will beat fossil fuels. Remember that about 20 percent of global electricity markets are paying more than $0.20 per kilowatt-hour, which is more than it cost Sungevity to serve electricity from a US rooftop in 2011 with a solar lease. I think that history will look back on this period and see that the tide turned in 2010 when fully half of new electric generation coming online globally was renewable. In the United States, renewables were 25 percent of new electric generation.

This sea change won't come to pass without a Rooftop Revolution, however. It won't happen magically (although the invisible hand will help out our side of the ledger) because fossil interests will use their power to resist it. And that's why we need to spawn a new heroic breed of entrepreneurs willing to make it happen—our New Greatest Generation, which will be willing to take up the fight while building businesses at the same time. And we need positive energy policies supported by solar citizens to demand that these changes happen, no matter what King CONG and its cronies say or do.

Solutions exist from A to Z: At Sungevity, for every home we lease solar to in the United States, we set up a solar lighting and charging solution for a family in Zambia so that kids there can read at night. In other examples of what needs to be done, export agencies have developed low-interest-rate programs with more than $100 billion in financing available for solar tech transfer and clean-technology deployment. Microfinancing and crowdfunding services such as Grameen Energy allow people to access these services with financing. Mobile billing and other innovations will extend the reach of sunshine into the lives of the more than 500 million people who have cell phones but no electricity in their homes. That's why Sungevity sponsors a solar lighting kit that doubles as a cell-phone charger—to get these people connected to the Internet and to the sun, two keys to twenty-first-century living.

The sky is the limit for this kind of technological and business ingenuity now that solar is cost-effective. The year 2012 has been designated by the United Nations as the International Year of Sustainable Energy for All, and the UN called on the world to focus on this opportunity to pull the world's poorest people from the unsafe and hazardous use of fossil-fuel energy and into a cleaner, better future. There are many great ways to do this; indeed, a world of opportunity exists at "the bottom of the pyramid" for solar entrepreneurs to do well while doing good. Furthermore, solar electricity is one of best anti-poverty measures around because, while energy poverty is only a piece of larger economic poverty, providing electricity is proven to be one of the best ways out of it. Light is education for people, and electricity is economic empowerment. This is truly what we mean by the Solar Ascent.

Why now? Because thanks to the solar industry, it's more affordable than ever, and you'll continue to save money on your electricity bill over the coming decades. In fact, going solar by 2015 will be economically rational for two-thirds of the households in the United States.

Forgive me for sounding like a broken record, but a couple of key things have happened recently: The cost of manufacturing the panels has decreased by more than 50 percent since 2010. That reduction in costs is passed on to the consumer in the price you pay today. Just as important is the fact that you can now lease the solar system rather than having to pay for the whole thing up front. As discussed earlier, paying for a solar system all at once is a bit like buying your energy for 25 years or buying a chunk of the coal-fired power plant rather than paying for your service contract with a utility. One of the big changes for the solar industry in recent years has been the third-party financing of our assets, which means we sell a service as well as a product. The solar lease is a real game changer.

The other reason why now is the right time to go solar is that we have made it easier. In the past, if you were interested in going solar, you had to research a local contractor, call him, and get him to come out to your house so he could climb on the roof to design a solar array—and then he would come back to try to sell you a paper-based proposal. There were a lot of scheduling issues and clunky cottage-industry customer experiences with solar in the past. As we've scaled, we've learned from other industries and made the buying experience much more convenient.

Sungevity as a Case in Point

To get a solid quote, Sungevity's customers fill out a simple online form, which includes identifying their home on a map interface for us. We then use a combination of satellite and aerial photography of the home to build a three-dimensional model and virtualize the deployment of solar panels on the roof. We do this to calculate the electricity production from the panels and thereby generate a firm quote, including the economics, for the installation of the solar panels in real life. Unlike with solar's mom-and-pop-shop experience of the past, we never have to climb up on your roof to tell you what it will involve to go solar.

With the magic of software combined with satellite and aerial imagery, we can do in a snap what it took human processes hours to complete. Then, as in so many other industries, from the replacement services for travel agencies (think Expedia) to those for video stores (Netflix), we serve up our core product, which is our solar proposal—or, as we call it, the iQuote—over the Internet. We e-mail it to you. Not only does this save us great cost in serving our customers but it's a scalable model, whereas driving trucks in traffic to serve millions of homes that should go solar is not. In 2011 we started a partnership with a company in the Netherlands, and we're now providing remote solar-design services for homes in that country, as well, which is a great development for the US solar industry.

I say it's a great development not just because the company I work for is doing this but because it's bringing easy and affordable solar to more people. Aside from cost savings and scalability, our online sunshine model, as we call it, creates a better customer experience. Perhaps my favorite story about this comes from our early prospecting in 2008, shortly after we had invented the remote solar-design process. We delivered fully engineered but paper-based iQuotes to homes in the San Francisco Bay Area that were appropriate for solar systems. On the mailer we provided a login and a password for our website that allowed people to learn more or to sign up for a solar system.

We were not expecting much response the week after we delivered these paper-based proposals, but suddenly our customer relationship management database told us that a customer had paid the deposit for a cash purchase. We hadn't had a phone call or even an e-mail from this person to ask us any questions about our proposal—just an order placed in our system. I was so excited that I had to find out who had just ordered the world's first online solar solution for his home. I was sure the customer was a savvy digital Gen X-er. When we phoned him, we discovered he was an octogenarian US Air Force veteran who wanted to do the right thing by his kids by going solar. He was happy to pay for it with cash because he felt the benefits were in his legacy. I savored the moment as a reminder to never assume anything; our first customer wasn't some slick, techie kid but instead one of our elders and betters showing the way.

Aside from that great experience, I'm proud of what we've done with remote solar design because it has broken the mold of the quoting process, which is a costly and cumbersome part of the sales cycle in the solar industry. To go back to that vision of two-thirds of American homes saving money by going solar, you start to get a sense of the scale of enterprise that's required to serve all of these people. Between 40 million and 50 million homes in the United States should go solar if the homeowner acts rationally from an economic point of view. To date, the industry has served approximately 200,000 homes, but this is changing—and what's now just a revolt is soon to become a revolution.

By making solar adoption easy and affordable, our industry can build trust and the base of reference customers to really grow to scale. As we know, the best indicator of what one consumer might do in the United States is what his or her neighbor is doing. At Sungevity we're proactively trying to cultivate what we like to call "peer pride." The good news is that this is relatively easy because going solar is a viral phenomenon, one in which customers are happy to be the contagion.

Two academics at Stanford University showed this virality with solar systems through a study of their installation in different ZIP codes. They concluded that for every 1 percent of new installations in an area, it was 1 percent faster for the next solar system to be installed in the same neighborhood. They attributed this to two causal factors: one was that there was greater customer acceptance of solar as a value proposition because "my neighbor was doing it" rather than "some crazy hippie" and, second, because the clerk down at City Hall would be more familiar with solar installations and would process the construction permit more quickly.

So we have fed what we call the "solar social network" with our tools and incentive systems. These are both monetary incentives and social incentives because people are happy to engage their community in the process of going solar. For example, I have a small nine-panel system on my home, and my next-door neighbor has one, and his other next-door neighbor has one, too—all from Sungevity. Last weekend I received a text from a neighborhood friend who watches my kid. She told me she was going to go solar with Sungevity because she had just gone to our website and found it all so easy and financially attractive. I joked with my friend that I'd pay my daughter a commission for the sale, but she said I didn't need to—it was just what everyone was doing on the block.

There goes the neighborhood! And this process will sweep suburbia in the coming years. Watch as your neighborhood disregards Dirty Energy's baloney and goes solar, for this is the home front in the epic struggle against King CONG, and the people are on our side. Now is the time to occupy our rooftops!

What You Can Do as a Rooftop Revolutionary

▶ Help set the record straight by challenging misinformation.
Directly question unbalanced and outright negative media
reports on the viability of solar power by sending a letter to
the editor, demanding accurate and balanced reporting on
energy issues.

▶ Educate your network of friends and colleagues about the truth
regarding Solyndra's failure and how it has been blown out of
proportion by King CONG and its allies in the media and used to
inaccurately depict the entire solar industry as a failure.

▶ Visit the Sungevity blog (blog.sungevity.com) when you need
clarity on energy issues. You can also send us your question via
our Facebook page (www.facebook.com/sungevity).

▶ Get the most current facts and talking points on the Solar
Ascent at www.rooftoprevolutionbook.com.

CHAPTER 5

Hot Jobs

The great economic revolutions in history occur when
new communications technologies converge with new
energy systems.

—JEREMY RIFKIN

FROM EDUCATORS TO WAR HEROES AND FROM ROCK STARS TO
everyday people, Americans are reaping the benefits of the Solar
Ascent and benefitting from the multitude of jobs it's quickly
and steadily creating.

Take Justin Cox, a bloody hero to me. He jumps out of air-
planes at altitudes so high that he's required to wear breathing
gear, and then he swoops down diagonally like a flying squir-
rel at seemingly impossible speeds toward a drop zone, pulls
his chute at the heart-stopping last minute, shoots upward, and
then floats down to land precisely on his target. He was a US
Army Special Forces operative on two tours of Iraq before he
suffered a serious head injury from a roadside bomb. Having
sat on a barstool across from him and listened to his stories, I
know he's been through things I'm glad I've never had to deal
with, and it's clear he's proved his valor and loyalty to the United
States many times over.

Justin is one of Sungevity's Southern California field managers, which means he oversees our installation operations in

that large market. Every day he drives around in an orange Prius, checking the safety of the rooftop crews and ensuring that we're doing high-quality work and that our customers are satisfied. He works tirelessly because we're installing solar systems on a lot of homes in the large area he covers, which includes Orange County and extends all the way down to the border with Mexico. His wife told me that she's happy, even though he spends long hours on the road, because he's safe now and doing something just as meaningful to him as his work in the army. Justin told me that he loves his job because he can see his family and take care of them, yet, as he has said, "I am still fighting for energy security."

Justin is just one example of the thousands of people who are getting into solar careers. Indeed, many veterans like him are coming home from foreign wars and finding a place in solar enterprises that use their skills and engage them in a growth industry that's doing right by the country. This industry is creating jobs and value for families as well as fostering independence from fossil fuels, which cost our nation blood and treasure. And the best news is that there are many more jobs to come.

The Reality of the Solar Employment Engine

Here are some statistics that illustrate the reality of this employment engine. From 2010 to 2011, the solar industry doubled, making it one of the fastest-growing sectors in the economy. More than 100,000 Americans now work in the industry—twice as many as in 2009 and almost twice the number of Americans working in coal mines. These Americans are staffing the approximately 5,600 solar companies that now exist in the United States, most of which are small businesses, where most of the growth in employment occurs in the economy—not in the big businesses of corporate America. What's more, these businesses now exist in all 50 states.

And we've also been doing well in the global game. The United States was a net exporter of solar products in 2010, the last year for which we have numbers, and we're likely to see that this trend continued in 2011. In 2010 we had a net surplus of $2 billion in solar products traded globally. We were even a net exporter to China, the world's solar giant, by more than $240 million. Solar energy is a global industry that benefits from open and fair markets, and the bottom line is that trade in solar products has been good for the United States by expanding export opportunities for domestic manufacturers, creating jobs, and driving down costs to consumers, which makes the product all the more accessible.

As discussed earlier, most jobs in the solar industry are not in manufacturing but in the sale, marketing, financing, and installation of these products, so the lower the manufacturing cost are, the more demand there will be for jobs in these other areas. There's a risk that our momentum will be lost, and many jobs with it, because of weak leadership, backward politics, and the repression of the Solar Ascent by the vested interests that oppose it—especially coal, nuclear, and gas-fired-electricity companies—so we have to demand that our leaders stay on the right path.

Although China is currently the big fish in solar-panel manufacturing, new US manufacturing facilities have begun operations in Arizona, Michigan, Mississippi, Ohio, Pennsylvania, and Tennessee. These are states that hemorrhaged jobs at the end of the 2000s due to the recession, and the solar industry has helped put communities in these states back to work. Not all of these companies will make it—some may have already fallen out—but that's the nature of an innovative sector trying something new in a struggling economy.

The Internet sector has had its failures (think Webvan and Pets.com), but let's not forget the myriad other Internet companies that have revolutionized the way we live. Solar manufacturing will continue to grow in the United States if the market-supporting policies for the deployment of its products are maintained. Global manufacturing companies, like GE and Kyocera, want to build their factories to be close to distribution channels in what many analysts expect will be the largest solar market in a few years, and this will become increasingly true as the cost of transport becomes a larger portion of the cost structure of the total solar solution. As the form factor of solar panels and other photovoltaic products changes, tapping the power of the sun in creative ways will give our workers a lot to do.

It's important to note how many jobs the Rooftop Revolution portends compared with those dependent on ol' King CONG. Despite a lack of sustained government support in the past decade, the overall advanced-energy economy—including wind, energy efficiency (like insulation and weather stripping), and solar—has added more than 770,000 jobs. By comparison the 100-year-old fossil-fuel sector—including utilities, coal mining, and oil and gas extraction (all industries that have received significant government subsidy)—had about 1.27 million workers in 2007, when this analysis was made. The numbers have probably changed a bit in the past five years but to clean energy's advantage, as oil and coal have shed jobs across America and our industry has grown. In other words, for all the history and the profits of King CONG's companies, they employ fewer than twice as many people as the clean-energy industry. The shift is under way, and it's going to be huge!

Remember that the bulk of the solar workforce will be outside the factory gates. As the solar industry grows, most of the direct employment is taking place in companies that market, sell, finance, install, and service solar installations. And the growth will continue if the positive energy policies needed to support it are maintained by the governments regulating electricity—especially our right to sell into the grid and the incentives for solar's deployment.

Holding Our Representatives to Account

One policy that's been a successful stimulator of the solar economy is a cash grants Treasury program for the tax credits that the solar industry has received. As we've discussed, most US energy-industry players receive subsidies in the form of tax credits. In the case of the solar industry, the industry tax credit administered by the Internal Revenue Service has a term that will end in 2016. This credit allows investors to write off 30 percent of the value of the solar systems they pay for. In 2009, as part of the effort to get the economy going again, the federal government converted this to a cash grant in lieu of tax credits, known as the 1603 Treasury Program.

This program changes the timing of when energy developers can claim incentives, by allowing them to take federal grants in lieu of their incentives later when they file their taxes. One positive effect of this change in timing is that it has provided the liquidity needed for further development of energy projects—think working capital for small businesses. It has truly been a success: as of the end of 2011, the 1603 Treasury Program has financed more than 22,000 solar projects around the country, totaling $1.5 billion, which drove more than $3.5 billion in private investments in 47 states. Overall the program has leveraged more than $22 billion in private-sector investment for a range of energy technologies in all 50 states. It sounds like the cash grant is a successful strategy, right?

So why are our representatives risking all of this job-creating momentum by allowing the program to expire? The cash grant basically fell victim to shenanigans in Congress at the end of 2011, when the House and the Senate couldn't agree to pass anything more than emergency spending bills. We've now forgotten the details of their petty fights, but among the collateral damage was a request to extend the 1603 Treasury Program that was left on the chamber floor. As a result, the tax equity market going into 2012 was uncertain, putting an additional 37,000 direct, indirect, and induced jobs at stake—the estimate of how many more people would be employed in the solar industry with a one-year extension of this one program.

To allow the program to lapse was akin to raising taxes on the solar industry—an action that would significantly hamper its growth. A survey of the US Partnership for Renewable Energy Finance estimates that the end of the cash grant program will shrink the total financing available for solar projects by 52 percent in 2012 alone—just as the demand for solar is increasing. Congress should have extended this policy that creates jobs in a technology-neutral manner without picking winners but encouraging the continued development of clean energy, which is what an increasing number of Americans want. We the People must exhort our politicians to stand with solar and support entrepreneurs who are finding a way to build their businesses and grow the solar economy, despite the on-again, off-again assistance from government.

While waiting for our elected officials to follow the will of the people, we can also vote with our feet, and indeed we are.

LinkedIn, which has some of the richest data about career paths and opportunities, was asked to analyze its 7 million US members who have switched industries during the past five years. The growth in the "Renewables and the Environment" category was 56.8 percent—almost off the chart. The Internet, online publishing, and wireless technology were the next closest, but these fields didn't beat 30 percent growth. Clean energy has the jobs of the present and the future.

Building the Solar Economic Ecosystem

To me, people joining the solar workforce are all rock stars in the figurative sense, but an example of someone who has joined the solar industry and is also literally a rock star is Rue Phillips, onetime guitarist for the heavy-metal band Black Sabbath. He now runs a company that cleans and maintains solar systems, and he's another hero of the Solar Ascent because his company is an early example of the ancillary services that will be a byproduct of the mass manufacture and deployment of solar panels.

Following his music career, Rue became an electrician, and while building a contracting business he had his eyes on solar, which he saw as an up-and-coming solution. Having been an indoor wireman in homes for a couple of decades, he knew the solar potential of the skin of residential buildings. He taught himself and his crews how to install solar systems while doing other electrical work in the residential sector, and he realized that a bigger opportunity would be managing them over time.

Even though the solar panel is very low maintenance, with no moving parts, it does need to be cleaned occasionally, and at times things do happen, like squirrels nesting under it or branches falling onto it. Furthermore, the inverter and some of the other components need maintenance from time to time, and as millions of these systems are installed, more of them will need annual service calls. So Rue took some risks, invested some of his own money to retool his crews and buy new trucks, and with a business partner built out True South Renewables, a company that's now dominant in several regions in providing operation and maintenance services to the solar industry.

At the start of 2012, two-year-old True South had more than 200 megawatts under contract and another 500 megawatts in negotiation, from Texas to Ontario and in quite a few US states in between. Rue's business services small rooftops and big utility-scale solar projects, with both big and small solar-panel arrays; but if all the deals he has in the works were single-family homes, there would be some 40,000 of them. In other words, his company will create a lot of jobs in the years to come as it provides what he calls "gold standard packages," which include a once-a-year audit, or check of the system; a panel washing; and 24-hour emergency tech callout service. True South could become the Geek Squad of solar—or even something bigger—very soon.

This is just one example of hundreds of creative companies springing up in the ecosystem surrounding the Rooftop Revolution. I'm on the board of The Solar Foundation, which conducts an annual census of solar job creation in the United States. This is a fairly perfunctory process of counting heads in companies—less modeling exercise or economic forecast than an actual census of people employed directly by the solar industry. It's from this National Solar Jobs Census that the Solar Energy Industries Association can claim 100,000 jobs now in the industry, which is a wonderful result for all Americans.

As a board member, however, I'm certain that the census underestimates the number of people who are actually employed in the industry because the association has some very stringent standards by which these numbers are calculated, and it also depends on the accuracy of the surveys submitted by industry company managers (we're all so busy that many of us likely haven't even filled out a census form). We estimate a much higher number of people employed in some states than currently shown in the job census, and in 2012 and beyond we'll be using an even more rigorous methodology to get accurate numbers for this growing US workforce.

What The Solar Foundation won't be able to show is indirect employment—the phenomenon that comes with the Solar Ascent. Indirect solar employment comes in the form of jobs that are tangentially linked to the Solar Ascent. And one big source of employment creation will be jobs that businesses large and small will be able to create when they have more money to spend—because as we've proved, solar electricity is cheaper than grid electricity. This may seem to contradict conventional wisdom, but, as we've already shown, the conventional wisdom of the Dirty Energy economy is not that wise; consider the idea of boiling water with uranium at Fukushima (an earthquake- and tidal-wave-prone area)—not a smart way to create electricity by any standard.

One example of the phenomenon of indirect job creation is in the schools sector of California. Some of the fastest uptake of solar panels in California has been in the public-sector-built environment because these institutions are hurting from energy costs and need the savings they can get by going solar. As of 2012, 114 megawatts of solar systems are already installed in California public-sector buildings, such as schools and government offices as well as other state-run facilities, and another 239 megawatts of applications are in process. The savings to California is greater than $1.3 billion! In a state that has a

$5 billion deficit, you can see the relative significance of the savings created by going solar. Schools are among the worst hit by the state's budget crisis, and a bright light for them is the savings they can realize by going solar. Of this savings, more than $800 million is expected to go to school districts and universities, freeing up resources to retain teachers and dampen budget cuts currently in process.

At a time when educators in our society are needed more than ever, $800 million pays a lot of salaries. And who would have thought that going solar at your kids' school could help stave off the scarcity thinking that has crept into our education system. As the bumper sticker says, "If you think education is expensive, try ignorance!" It's my hope that more state government entities will move to solar; and with the projects already under application—between 70 and 130 megawatts—more solar will be installed in 2012, with a net projected lifetime savings of $300 million to $700 million. These are just some of the benefits that accrue from embracing the solar economy.

SunPower Corporation, based in San Jose, California, is one of the companies most involved in the school sector of the Rooftop Revolution. It has installed solar systems for 90 school districts across the state, using mostly union labor. This is a 25-year-old company and one of the giants of the US solar industry, with more than 1,000 employees in offices and manufacturing facilities throughout the country. Many of the people whom SunPower employs directly have careers common in the solar industry: PhD scientists, lawyers, accountants, engineers, market analysts, manufacturing employees and installers, salespeople, and customer service representatives.

The company also has 400 independent dealer-partners in 300 cities in 42 states—that's more than 6,000 indirect jobs, by

SunPower's calculation. In its supply chain are 26 US companies that deliver materials like polysilicon and glass as well as inverters and other system components. SunPower's factory in Milpitas, California, contracts with plants in Colorado, Illinois, Oregon, and Pennsylvania to build its equipment. The multiplier effect is hard to quantify, but keep in mind that employees typically return 28 percent of their salaries in local, state, and federal taxes, according to the US Department of Labor's Bureau of Labor Statistics. And then these workers spend 36 percent of their salaries on goods and services in the local economy. So the success of SunPower has effects beyond lower-cost electricity, a reduction in pollution, and the teachers' jobs that it saves.

If you're wondering whether all this employment generated by solar-power systems causes the cost of these systems to go up, you can rest easy because that's not the case: employment cost is factored into the price of the electricity we get from the solar systems. We have the Solar Ascent to thank for employing so many people in a country with such high unemployment while producing a critical service commodity at a decreasing price over time.

Keep in mind that the price per kilowatt-hour is going down while the number of employees is going up. This is because renewable-energy systems are more job-dense than their fossil-fuel-energy equivalents by a significant factor, depending on the type of fuel and its application. In the jargon of economists, solar power is "relatively labor-intense" due to the wide variety and the larger number of jobs required in installation, maintenance, construction, and so on. In an analysis of the literature on the subject, academics at UC Berkeley determined that renewable-energy technologies create more jobs per average megawatt of power generated and per dollar invested in construction, manufacturing, and installation than does the processing of coal or natural gas.

Over a 10-year period, the solar industry created 5.65 jobs per million dollars invested, whereas the entire coal-fired power generation chain produces only 3.96 jobs per million dollars sunk into it. Put head to head against coal mining, solar produced 40 percent more employment per dollar invested. That means we get more jobs and less poison when we get electricity straight from the sun.

Where will the solar jobs come from in an economy that's going to be tough for at least a few more years? Most of the growth will be in sales and distribution—34 percent year over year. Installation employment numbers are projected to grow 22 percent in 2012 compared with 2011, while manufacturing will grow 14 percent. Can you imagine any of those growth rates in almost any other economic sector?

We usually celebrate such steep growth with much fanfare, no matter how small the starting point may be. But that's not always the case when it comes to solar. Take General Electric's solar plans. At around the same time that Solyndra went bust in late 2011, GE announced plans to buy a startup solar manufacturer and build a factory using its technology. The plant is going to be in Colorado and will employ about 400 people there, plus another 100 or so who will support the solar business at GE's famous research campus in Schenectady, New York. The factory will be bigger than 11 football fields and supply enough panels to power about 80,000 homes each year. GE expects to build similar plants around the world as the industry grows.

Remember, GE is the company that generalized electricity, and it is pretty serious about being a big part of the solar economy. I used to love the chorus of the Midnight Oil song "When the Generals Talk":

> When the generals talk
> You better listen to him
> When the generals talk
> You better do what he say!

Well, this is GE's statement: "We are all in. We are going to invest what it takes . . . because we know that by 2020 this is going to be at least a $1 billion product line." This was said by GE's Jeff Immelt (who also happens to head Obama's Jobs Council). "I don't care about Solyndra or any of that other stuff; we did this with no government funding. We can do this."

Job Growth—but Only If We Demand It

There really is no question that the Solar Ascent will create lots of jobs. The only question is, *Will mainstream America benefit from them?* We know that the people want them: for four consecutive years, nine out of 10 Americans have said they "think it is important" for the United States to develop and use solar energy.

Perhaps a more concrete proof point was the hardball campaign that led to the 20-point rejection of California's Proposition 23 (as discussed in chapter 3): Texas Oil's attempt to stop California's emerging clean-energy economy in its tracks. The significance of Prop 23's lopsided defeat was that it challenged the mythology that clean energy was somehow at odds with creating new jobs. In our sound-bite world, if you assert something and put enough dollars behind it, it often starts to be accepted as the truth—and that's what Big Oil was counting on. But it didn't succeed in this case, and voters signaled en masse that they know the truth. Despite the ongoing trauma of having more unemployed workers than any other state in the nation, Californians voted by a large margin to support clean energy in 2010. Why? Poll after poll shows that voters' foremost concern is jobs. Could it be that voters see the twofold growth of new jobs sprouting from the clean economy over the rest?

Creating Smart Jobs in the Solar Space

We know that people who are changing careers are moving into the renewables and environment space faster than in any other industry. The *Wired* magazine article "The Economic Rebound: It Isn't What You Think" analyzed job creation coming out of the recession. The publication concluded that the economy is not just gaining jobs as it slowly rebounds but also creating a new category of middle-class work that it called "smart jobs": "They're innovative and high tech, but most of them are located far from Silicon Valley or New York. They're specialized, but that doesn't mean you need a PhD or even (in some cases) a college degree to get them or to do them well—though they do require some serious training, whether on the job or in a vocational program."

A lot of solar jobs, and some of the ancillary work or adjacent enterprises spawned by the Rooftop Revolution, match the profile of these smart jobs. They blur the line between conventional blue-collar and white-collar work. These jobs can involve working in a factory, but those workers are using more brains than brawn. This kind of work is cropping up all over the country and is not confined to one industry or geographical region. As pockets of innovation gain a foothold, these jobs will grow and employers will multiply.

Clean tech and computers create the perfect storm for this sort of economic transformation. The nexus between these two markets—called the CleanWeb, by some—is as huge an area of growth as any in the economy. I believe the combination of software and the momentum of the Solar Ascent is going to generate enormous value and employment in coming years.

At Sungevity we created a new category of worker, the remote solar designer. Prior to our company's creation of software that combined aerial and satellite images to allow accurate engineering of a solar-panel solution for a home without going to the site, this job was done manually. Now we have about 20 people fulfilling this function, so there's no driving in traffic to get to the houses to take some measurements and draft a proposal for an installation. As mentioned, we even size homes in the Netherlands and design solutions for Dutch customers, half a world away from our office in Oakland, California.

The time and cost savings from this approach are obvious, and the efficiency has led to hypergrowth in our business that allows us to employ even more people. I like to think we're also saving lives because we're placing fewer people on roofs than would otherwise be required—and each time you get on a hazardous job site, you're taking risks. More technologies like this will be created to save time, money, and lives to proliferate solar in the Rooftop Revolution.

At least one exciting example for further job creation is the ingenious web-enabled commerce possible with Solar Mosaic, introduced in chapter 3. This is a crowdfunding platform for solar project developers: you go to a website either to invest in a solar project or to set up a "mosaic" that can be capitalized by other people coming to the site to invest and buy a piece, or "tile," in your solar project.

This kind of business is booming—ePropser and Lending Club, which are peer-to-peer lending variations on the theme, each move hundreds of millions of dollars per year. And like eBay a decade ago and Kiva in the developing world, these crowdfunding platforms will give all kinds of people the opportunity to build their own small businesses—in this case a solar project that makes money from the electricity it generates.

As Republican Senator Scott Brown of Massachusetts said in Congress in late 2011, crowdfunding "has the potential to be a powerful new venture capital model for the Facebook and Twitter age and its potential to create jobs is enormous." Crowdfunding is an online path for small businesses to grow, yet, as the senator noted, "the world right now is built around big business."

But small businesses of fewer than 500 people represent 99 percent of all employer firms in the United States. They employ half of all private-sector employees and created 65 percent of net new jobs in the past 20 years. Of high-tech workers, 43 percent are in small businesses as scientists, engineers, programmers, and so on. Information technology meets energy technology—IT and ET—and makes for the business models that matter in recovering from the Great Recession and spawning our New Greatest Generation.

The disruption of the energy and the finance worlds, linked with local, social, and mobile software and an information layer to existing infrastructure, will be enormous. The Information Age has transformed nearly every other industry on the planet, but as energy consumers we're still constricted by nineteenth-century energy sources and business models. In our electricity-generating infrastructure, we need serious innovation, which has stagnated, to refocus on this nexus; and our talented technologists should be doing meaningful—even epic—engineering on the level of the first Greatest Generation, which got us to the moon.

There should be a thousand great ideas coming out of the CleanWeb every month. The declining costs of solar cells and panels will lead to lots of new uses—such as replacing dirty diesel generators and accelerating the demand for microgrids around local, clean power. Some of these may be "virtualized," which means they use software to aggregate multiple sources to help make these largely invisible and decentralized power sources more valuable to utilities and grid operators. Think of the way some computing is done by networked machines (rather than one big supercomputer). Coordinating this infrastructure evolution into smooth service will require the imagination and the skills at which American ingenuity excels.

I subscribe to the theory that the retail electricity market in homes and businesses will be turned on its head in the next few years by new technologies and that smaller players selling clean electricity will be better positioned than the large incumbents with their dirty power. This is because the future of the electricity business is on the house, rather than out front on a pole in the street. In the new scenario of the sunshine mesh, utility companies would give up some of their traditional top-down control over both the supply and the transmission of electricity to become, at least partially, an integral part of an electricity network involving thousands of small energy producers. In this scheme the utility company would become the manager of the energy Internet. Its profit model moves increasingly away from selling its own energy to becoming a service provider, using its expertise and infrastructure to manage other people's energy.

But to get to this ideal state, corporations and society need a push. Entrepreneurs in all forms can do a lot of the work. Much of the rest will be done by solar citizens supporting our New Greatest Generation. It's time that those of us who believe we can forge our future should stop talking and start *doing*. It's the only way to get the global economy and our planet back on track. In short we can all be educators, heroes, and rock stars in the Solar Ascent.

What You Can Do as a Rooftop Revolutionary

▶ Be a worker for the Rooftop Revolution by joining the solar workforce. Visit www.solarworksforamerica.org and other such sites, such as www.solarjobs.us, where you can explore employment opportunities.

▶ Support The Solar Foundation (www.thesolarfoundation.org), a nonprofit organization that demonstrates the global benefits of solar energy and issues the annual National Solar Jobs Census.

▶ If you work for a larger company, be a solar intrapreneur by urging your employer to get involved in the Solar Ascent. Partner with co-workers to fund a community solar project at www.solarmosaic.com.

CHAPTER 6

Energized

> People have always been good at imagining the end of
> the world, which is much easier to picture than the strange
> sidelong paths of change in a world without end.
>
> —REBECCA SOLNIT, FROM *HOPE IN THE DARK:*
> *UNTOLD HISTORIES, WILD POSSIBILITIES*

JOURNEY BACK WITH ME TO 1989, TO THE SOUTHERN HIGH-
lands of Papua New Guinea. I'm 19 years old. I'm bird watch-
ing and bumming around this magnificent land, working as a
trekking guide among the country's indigenous people. A road
called the Highlands Highway, which had been built just a
year before, snakes through forest, where clouds of butterflies
explode from fragrant bushes and stunning birds of paradise
display each evening as the dirt strip winds down into Tari. I've
spent the past three months hiking around the valley, stopping
at each village along the way to meet the people.

Big Oil companies, led by BP, had recently come to the valley to drill, with little regard for how their work would affect the
inhabitants. Their presence ignited a Wild West–like frenzy in
the region.

Let us in and we'll give you electricity was part and parcel of
the promise of these Western companies.

Electricity. The people had heard of it—its mysterious, magical power. They wanted it. Some of them grew obsessed with the prospect of such technology and the fortune they thought it could bring.

Crazy stuff was happening. In one part of the valley, an incredible landslide had occurred a few years before. Half of an enormous mountain collapsed, revealing a glittering field of gold. A gold rush ensued. One local kid found nuggets the size of his thumbnails and used one to buy a Toyota Land Cruiser in the nearest town, hundreds of kilometers away, though he had no idea how to drive. He ended up driving it off a road and killing himself. This was a people who had never seen a wheel until the first airplane landed among them in the 1930s. This was a Stone Age culture catapulted into the Space Age. I worked with a helicopter pilot who dropped live chickens in nets to the miners, who groped at the air below us to catch them for their dinner.

Not all of the region's people believed in the promise of BP and all this magic that "business" was going to bring to the place. One night I was taken up to a spot overlooking the entire Tari Valley, close to where the Hides gas fields were, to see BP's machinery roaring, dinosaur-like. There was an ancient myth among the local Huli people that a great snake had long ago gone into hibernation beneath the land, and when the monster finally woke and its eyes burned into the night, the end of the world was near. "Look," said one old man over the din, pointing to two searing points of light from the construction area, where heaps of land had been overturned, "the eyes of the snake!"

The hope for electricity was false. The gas pumped out of the ground wasn't the kind that generated electricity in a place like this; instead it was sucked away down a pipe. The people remained in the dark, except for the two bright lights in the night up on the hill at Hides.

These folks deserved better. They deserved electricity service, no doubt, and all the benefits it brings. But they didn't deserve the despoliation of their sacred home for fossil-fuel extraction, which not only wouldn't benefit them but would destroy their lifestyle. I remember looking up and feeling the sun's heat blanketing the Earth, so much of it that in a single hour it could fuel the Huli people's energy needs for a century. Thus my love affair with the sun began.

Two decades later I'm half a world away from Papua New Guinea. I'm now an entrepreneur in the center of the entrepreneurial universe—the San Francisco Bay Area—but I'm still in love with the sun and all the people who live under it, and I'm more confident than ever that the sun's power will win over Dirty Energy. Why?

Let's look into my crystal ball (solar powered, of course) and take a glimpse into the future. In the next decade, our world is going to see a massive increase in electricity generation, about 50 percent more than we have today, according to most forecasts (from the International Energy Agency's to Greenpeace's) and depending on how much of our vehicle fleet moves toward electrification. A small part of this new electricity generation will be to replace retired plants, but most of it will be an entirely new power infrastructure to meet the needs of the economically developing world. The United States itself will re-up more than 25 percent of the electricity-generating capacity for its own needs in the coming decade, while China will add 300 percent as much to its.

If we use coal to fuel this ramp-up, we're all cooked—figuratively and literally. It's simple carbon logic: if that much coal is dug up and burned to meet our ever-growing energy appetite, the carbon dioxide produced will raise the temperature of the Earth beyond safe levels. We can avert some of this fate by covering our buildings with solar panels.

In 2011 solar panels made up about 10 percent of new additions in the electricity market. So if we maintain that rate over the next decade, we'll install at least another 200 gigawatts—enough to cover 40 million homes. As we discussed at the beginning of the book, some people believe this is a conservative estimate. GE chief Jeff Immelt thinks India and China alone will install 200 gigawatts of solar power. These numbers are buoying investor confidence in the future of solar like never before. As noted, solar will likely grow even faster for one basic reason: economics are better for solar panels than for any other electricity generator because the massive scale of their manufacture makes them more affordable each year and because of new techniques that make them more powerful.

To give you a sense of the scaling effect of how rapidly solar power is growing, consider these numbers: In 1971, when I was born, less than 1 megawatt of solar panels was being produced each year globally. It wasn't until I was seven years old that we crossed the 1-megawatt-per-annum production threshold. It took another five years, into my tweens, to get to 10 megawatts-per-annum production. In 1997, the year I got married, the world passed the 100-megawatts-per-annum marker in the production of solar panels. In 2004 we had the capacity to produce 1 gigawatt (1,000 megawatts) per year, and just six years later we got to 10 gigawatts of production per annum. By 2014 the industry expects to produce 25 gigawatts of manufacturing capacity of solar panels each year. This is the equivalent of what two dozen of the largest-scale gas-, nuclear-, or coal-fired power plants can produce, but these power plants would cost more, take years to build, and require dirty fuel, whereas solar requires no fuel at all. Meanwhile, in January 2012 Sungevity installed 1 megawatt of solar panels—way more from a single new company in a single winter's month than was produced each year by the entire industry when I was born!

The rising cost of fuel is the Achilles' heel for Dirty Energy in the United States, and costs will continue to rise. Coal—the worst of the bunch—is becoming more expensive even though it's the most abundant. There are a number of reasons for this: In the United States, the productivity of coal mines peaked in 2000 and has decreased rapidly since. Most of our coal now comes from the Powder River Basin, in Wyoming, and parts of the Appalachians. The eastern coalfields are largely tapped out, so we're going to have to keep finding other sites to mine. Wyoming has a big transport bottleneck problem, and the cost to transport coal out of the Powder River Basin is three times that of mining it. This is due to the rising costs of the oil that the diesel locomotives need to haul the coal trains. The net result is that the price of coal delivery to American power plants grew three times faster than the rate of inflation between 2006 and 2011; therefore the states most dependent on coal had the highest electricity price increases.

Other parts of the cost structure of conventional electricity systems will also drive up the price of steam-based electricity over the coming decade, in particular transmission systems, which will require hundreds of billions of dollars of investment by the utilities that manage them—and guess who this cost is going to get passed on to. Yes, you, the customer.

Yet another reason for the rising price of fossil-fuel electricity is the byproducts of burning fossil fuels, otherwise known as pollution. Scrubbing pollution out of smokestacks, controlling mercury-contaminated ash, and attempting to capture and store carbon dioxide—all are adding to the liability side of the ledger for fossil-fuel power plants.

In my crystal ball, I see that over the next decade—as communities continue to be freaked out by weird weather; as mounting insurance costs drive Big Business to pay higher premiums; and as policymakers try to keep up with disasters, infrastructure impacts, and myriad other elements of climate change adaption—our country will start progressively imposing charges on Dirty Energy for carbon pollution, just as we've held the tobacco industry responsible for the impact of its products on the health of our communities. We've imposed taxes and regulations on Big Tobacco companies to reduce the impacts of the gaseous byproduct of burning tobacco and used the proceeds to pay for public health education, prevention, and treatment of smoking-related illness. This is the model of the carbon tax that Australia is imposing: take $20 per ton of carbon dioxide produced and create a fund to support clean energy over time. Makes sense to me. How about you?

Although our surgeon general is not making the case for clean energy in Congress, it's likely that, as slow as they are, our leaders will put a price on carbon because a growing number of us know that we have an option: solar energy. Historians have noted that the antislavery movement grew much of its support around the time that steam-engine technology was becoming known around the world for its ability to displace cheap human labor. People of the time needed a working alternative before they could make the shift away from the terrible centuries-old tradition of human bondage. Now we have an alternative to the dirty energy that's unjustly polluting our present and threatening our future, and that alternative is clean, renewable solar power.

Until now we've been beholden to the carbon pollution–producing technology to which we've become accustomed. But now that we have the reality of solar-panel and other clean-energy technologies in our midst, we must demand that our government and the corporations abandon the diabolic machinery of Dirty Energy. We as rooftop revolutionaries must clear our minds of the fog (or, more appropriately, FUD) that CONG has put into our heads and, like the slavery abolitionists, tell truth to power.

A *New York Times Magazine* writer who came to Sungevity in early 2012 to tour the office and find out what we were up to admitted that he knew nothing of the energy industry and was shocked to learn how competitive solar power had become. What he found out from his visit was so different from what he'd read in articles, from pieces in the *Washington Times* to *Wired*, about the ease and the affordability of going solar. At least this gentleman was trying to get to the truth.

The ignorance of most journalists and their lack of energy politics and policy coverage are the less impressive parts of their recent history. Some of this ignorance is understandable, given the level of propaganda we're all exposed to by the fossil-fuel industry. It's the gullibility with which they write up current history that gets me going.

Alec Guettel, one of my Sungevity partners, handles this issue well when briefing politicians and pundits. He points to the graph presented in chapter 1 that compares the historic price of grid electricity—predominantly supplied with fossil-fuel power—with the price of solar power. The graph shows electricity from the grid going up for more than a century as the price of solar declines precipitously from the middle of the timeline when it was invented. Alec then asks what the misunderstanding is. "I don't want to insult your critical thinking," he says, "but the fossil-fuel and utility industries represented by that line of growing revenues are among the richest and most profitable companies in history. Literally—in the history of the world. They have a lot of money to spend. And they don't like the look of this graph. And that's why they're generating a large amount of flak and deception."

Ol' King CONG has been threatened by these curves because the writing is on the wall; solar will become the lowest-cost source of electricity, and then CONG will have to resist market forces to maintain its thrall over electricity consumers and their money. They're using fear, uncertainty, and doubt as a form of procrastination. As the French wag Henri Queuille said, "Politics is the art of postponing decisions until they are no longer relevant." King CONG is trying to play waiting-game politics with our energy choices, but clean energy matters too much, and when there's so much at stake these choices will become more relevant every day.

And why should we wait? Solar adoption is upon us because of the true viability of the technology and people's growing enthusiasm for it. With products like the solar lease in the residential sector and other easy pay-as-you-go ways to tap the power of the sun, we're on the verge of the Solar Ascent.

10 Reasons Why the Solar Ascent Is Inevitable

To wrap it up, here are the 10 key reasons why I believe we're about to get our time in the sun.

1. Price

It bears repeating that solar power has become the lowest-cost source of electricity in many places. This has become obvious in island economies that were once completely dependent on diesel fuel to generate electricity. But it's also true in many retail electricity markets like the one you're part of when you pay the bill from your local power company. Already companies like Sungevity and others like it create an immediate savings for homes and businesses across the country. It's true in whole-sale markets too: in California the solar company SunPower has more than 700 megawatts under contract to connect to the utility grid, with prices below the cost of gas-based electricity. Energy isn't a winner-take-all market, but solar will be a big part of it. The bottom line is that solar will undercut new nuclear, coal, and gas plants in most parts of the country by the time those new plants could even be built because of solar power's rapid cost reduction.

2. Jobs

There are several times as many jobs per megawatt hour in the production of solar electricity as in the coal- or gas-fired steam-power industry. Millions of people worldwide are employed in the solar industry today. With the right policy support, the number of people employed could double each year or two, which means we have leverage in addressing unemployment both in the United States and overseas.

It's not easy to launch the businesses that create these jobs, and uncertainty in the policy settings and the financial environment add risk, but it's clear that the solar industry has the potential to be a major employer well into the twenty-first century.

As coal continues to shed jobs in the mining sector, and the capital-intensive fossil-fuel power-plant industry fails to engage more workers, solar power will become an attractive option for policymakers because it offers a wide range of job opportunities throughout the industry, not only in the factories but also beyond them—jobs that can't easily be off-shored, especially in sales, service, and maintenance.

3. Speed

The fastest-growing energy source on Earth, solar had a compounded annual growth rate of more than 40 percent for the first 10 years of the twenty-first century. Although growth cooled in 2011 because of fiscal trouble in Europe, and may slow down further for a few more years due to fallout from the Great Recession, this figure is incredible in any industry by any measure, especially as our economy is still struggling to get back on its feet. This is also why, though comparatively small in total numbers installed to date, solar panels represent the biggest threat to the fossil-fuel industry and the biggest hope for a carbon-free electricity industry.

It's surprising what an exponential curve will do! Based on current trends, solar power will be the salvation of our current nineteenth-century electricity grid and will constitute the lion's share of energy for the coming generation. I reckon that solar power in the United States will become more than a 10-gigawatt market by 2015 and jump to tens of millions of homes or household equivalents by 2020. Since 1992, according to the UN report "Keeping Track of Our Changing Environment," the historic rate of solar growth (30,000 percent) has actually exceeded that of Internet (29,000 percent) and cell phone

(23,000 percent) adoption, which is why I am confident that the true takeoff of the technology has only just begun.

4. Scalability

Although it can take five to seven years to build a gas or coal power plant in the United States, and decades to build a nuclear plant, it takes only months to install gigawatts of solar-power capacity. In 2010 three times as much solar-power capacity as nuclear-power capacity was installed worldwide. This was before the Fukushima disaster in Japan, which has effectively iced the building and the financing of these dangerous plants. Coal power plants are suffering a similar stigma because of the costs of pollution control associated with them. Large-scale solar still has some siting issues to contend with, but the Lego-like technology of solar is ultimately what makes it so scalable. Just look at a solar-paneled rooftop, which gets power at the point of use, and you'll probably see why it's better than building large central-station coal or nuclear power plants that come with such cost and risk.

5. Access

Solar power is now easy and affordable for many people. The commodity nature of solar panels has resulted in successful innovations in the business models that deliver energy to the community. The most exciting uptake is occurring throughout the economically developing world, where people don't have stable electricity supplies. New pay-as-you-go solar-power models have liberated people with clean, affordable lighting and charging solutions. Now these people are empowered both figuratively and literally.

The most pressing opportunity for solar entrepreneurs is in the world's economically challenged areas, where people are suffering from diesel fumes from generators they can ill afford just to get scraps of electric light—or, worse, using dangerous kerosene for fuel inside their homes—despite the economic reality that solar lighting is cheaper. We'll have to fight some dumb, negative energy polices to get electricity to these populations.

For example, $88 billion is paid from the budgets of 11 of the world's poorest countries for kerosene and diesel subsidies, according to the IEA and the International Institute for Sustainable Development. The air pollution caused by diesel and kerosene is killing these people and barely providing them the electricity service that the rest of us take for granted. We can do better than this. According to the IEA's analysis, it would be possible to achieve universal energy access for the world by 2030 with about $48 billion per year in global investment. That's half of what we spend on the obscene kerosene and diesel subsidies! "Solar is going to play a huge role in improving energy access," says Fatih Birol, the chief economist at the IEA.

Solar entrepreneurs can fill the need for the people of the world who don't have access to electricity as we do. At least $2 trillion to $5 trillion will be spent on energy worldwide in the coming two decades. Assume that only 20 to 25 percent of it is spent on distributed energy solutions, which include solar power and all other clean energy, battery storage, demand-side management, and energy efficiency improvements; it's $1 trillion, at least, that these solar entrepreneurs are playing for.

The solar lease has had a similarly disruptive impact on the solar market in the United States. Whereas it was not an option five years ago to pay for your system over time with no deposit, it's now the most common way to go solar. More than 60 percent of the US residential solar market in 2011—the biggest year ever—benefited from this creative customer finance solution. Now that people can pay for their solar power in installments, it's set to spread like wildfire, just like the adoption of Dish TVs and other home improvement services.

6. Value

All energy programs are subsidized, but solar power returns the best value of all energy subsidy programs. Fossil-fuel-based steam power has received at least $72 billion in subsidies over the past decade, and yet electricity prices have risen by about one-third. At the same time, solar-panel companies received single-digit billions in subsidies from the US government while their prices dropped by more than half. If the solar industry had the same kind of subsidy support that the fossil-fuel and nuclear industries received in the first five decades of their respective emergences, solar power would already be far cheaper and much more widely spread. With it would come more jobs, greater consumer savings, and a leadership role in the technology set that would dominate the energy industry in the twenty-first century and beyond.

7. Climate

Combined with wind and energy efficiencies, solar is our best fix for climate change. I hope by now you understand this threat and the moral imperative to reduce global warming, so I won't dwell on the need to get back to a safe level of carbon dioxide in the atmosphere by midcentury; rather I'll assume that that's the goal and that our civilization will come to its senses. Our best option to achieve this target comes from accelerating energy efficiency and demand-side management to reduce our use of electricity while displacing the supply coming from stored solar power in the form of fossil-fuel steam-based power plants with wind and solar electricity. It's the only broad formula that gets us to safe carbon levels, which also allows us to maintain our quality of life and spread electricity services to the billions of people without it.

Residential solar adoption is critical to the success of the Rooftop Revolution because it can help people understand how electricity works and what they can do to control it. This is the truly emancipatory potential in solar power to overthrow ol' King CONG. As social pressure grows, governments will act to employ local, clean energy. It's about positive energy policies, not politics.

8. Popularity

I'm of Irish descent, and for me there's no greater blessing than the famous Irish one: to have the sun shine warmly upon my face. So it is for most people, and so it is that when they can use the sun to power their homes and their lives, and discover how easy, affordable, and moral it is to do that, they'll spread the word. They'll tell their family, friends, and neighbors about it—over the fence, during backyard barbecues, and via social media—and these people will become energized themselves. There's a domino effect statistically evident in neighborhoods where homes have already gone solar, and this will perpetuate with time because solar adoption is easy, it's the right thing to do, and it's better for all.

9. Defense

If popularity is too fruity a justification for you, how about some cold, hard military brass for a reality check? The Department of

Defense (DOD) and our armed services love solar power. The DOD's clean-energy investments grew more than 300 percent from 2006 to 2009 and are projected to continue at that clip through 2030. What's in it for them? A safe, ubiquitous supply of sunlight—available from the United States to the mountains of Afghanistan and the deserts of Iraq—that doesn't need to be transported in vulnerable truck convoys or shipments and which, indeed, can reduce the "need" for a global military reach due to reduced dependence on imported fuel. You might be surprised to know that some of the highest casualty rates among our troops in the past decade were sustained while protecting diesel shipments used to air-condition tents in our foreign wars; and the greatest risks of war to date with more countries relate to petroleum or nuclear power, from North Korea to Iran. In other words, solar power keeps the peace.

10. Evolution

Solar-power adoption represents a new stage in the evolutionary ascent of humanity. Ultimately, people will evolve from our current steam-driven status quo to a more sustainable solar-powered civilization. Climate change doesn't mean the end of the world, but it does portend a lot of suffering the longer we allow it to continue. Given that the world will live on for many generations after our generation is gone, we have a responsibility to go solar now.

Humans have great and sometimes very timely ingenuity that has been applied to societal problems before, such as ending asbestos use and battling ozone depletion. Few of these problems have been as large as the threat of the climate destabilization, caused by our entrenched addiction to burning fossil fuels, but we do have a track record of averting disaster by adopting a new model when an old one becomes obsolescent. I'm confident that we'll adopt solar power as the new model.

But we still have a lot of work to do to be good ancestors, and our immediate descendants will have to continue our legacy to ensure the survival and the prosperity of our planet and all of its inhabitants. We're the New Greatest Generation, forging a Rooftop Revolution to pave the way for our *next* New Greatest Generation, who will see the Solar Ascent through. We must take the next steps. The science is in, the benefits are many, and the time to act is now.

"Look, the eyes of the snake!" said that old man two decades ago and half a world away, pointing to the destruction that ol' King CONG had wrought on his land and fearing that the end of the world was nigh. But now we don't have to look into the chasm, the gaping wound in the Earth. Instead we can turn our gaze upward, to the healing power of the sun—and see a world without end. Shine on!

What You Can Do as a Rooftop Revolutionary

▶ Educate your children about the power of the sun and solar energy. Get a solar grasshopper at www.rooftoprevolution book.com/kids. Watch your children's eyes light up when, as if by magic, the grasshoppers come to life when placed in sunlight.

▶ Provide light to the underprivileged and energy-deprived children in Zambia by donating a solar charging kit through http://www.sungevity.com/everychildhasalight.

▶ Sign your copy of this book on the inside back cover and pass it on to someone else who should read it.

Fire 2.0
My Ride on the Solar Coaster—So Far

> Never doubt that a small group of thoughtful, committed citizens can change the world; indeed, it's the only thing that ever has.
>
> —MARGARET MEAD

I'M AN ACTIVIST AND AN ENTREPRENEUR. I'VE FOUND THAT when people discover this, certain descriptions pop into their heads: *revolutionary, game changer, world changer, mover and shaker, troublemaker, fool,* and *Richard Simmons.* That's right, I was recently described as "the Richard Simmons of solar" in a blog post flaming solar businesses, and I took it as a compliment; like the fitness guru, I'm an unabashedly enthusiastic activist for my industry. Plus I have curly hair.

I've been an activist most of my life—since I was 12 years old, in fact. We jumped around a lot during my childhood—from Los Angeles to Chicago, then to Australia when I was three, and then back to LA until I was nine. After that it was off to London for a couple of years. I was 11 by the time we had settled again in Sydney, that sunny seaside city that makes me think of blue skies and beautiful beaches. A restless young stranger in this town, I fell in with a group of volunteers at the Australian Conservation Foundation in the Rocks district downtown. The foundation's and other groups' purpose was to block the construction of a dam in Tasmania, a project that would threaten that gorgeous island's massive wilderness.

Our goal was to get the federal government to oppose the building of the dam, which, through our electoral efforts, it did—thus blocking the construction and, more importantly, spawning the Australian Greens Party, which to this day holds the balance of power in the Federal and Tasmanian Parliaments. It was my first taste of victory as a global citizen—and my first realization of the power we have. This is what we can make happen by galvanizing our friends, sending out letters, organizing rallies, leveraging the media, talking to cameras, shouting loudly, joining minds and hands, voting, and working in unison for a common cause.

After that there was no stopping me. Forest campaigns in the mainland wilderness of New South Wales were my main thing until the late eighties, when I got active on "atmosphere issues" such as global warming and ozone depletion.

When I was holding up signs at big mining-company meetings, or physically protecting forests from destruction, or throwing my body under police vans, or climbing hundreds of feet up in the air to hang a protest banner—all with the aim of stopping Big Business from doing harm to people and the planet in the name of profit—I'd often hear some distant, disembodied voice shouting at me, "Get a job, you bum!" And I always laughed because most of the blokes saying it don't have a clue about how grueling a job effecting social change really is.

I've dug my elbows and belly into gravel in acts of civil disobedience, and I've spoken at corporate meetings on behalf of an order of nuns who were shareholders in a mining company but wanted to stop its environmental and human-rights abuses (we were met by the heckles of board members, including Henry Kissinger!). Efforts like these made for a harder day's labor than a lot of those I've experienced as a businessman. Down Under they call this "yakka," and activists as well as Aussies know what that means: hard work.

Now that I'm not only an activist but also an entrepreneur—the type of job creator those hecklers might have had in mind as a suitable pursuit—I find that my life hasn't changed very much at all: hard yards and lots of change. As an activist, you have to have passion, you have to be fearless, you have to be willing to take risks, and most of all you have to believe that you can change the world. You also have to be at least a little bit crazy. These same traits I've found to be useful in entrepreneurship as well.

Making the Leap from Activism to Entrepreneurialism

So the obstinate mind-set that led me to activism seems to suit me just fine as an entrepreneur. And this mind-set served me well as I embarked on the endeavor that would become Sungevity. Deciding to make the leap from activism to business in 2006 wasn't really tough at all; I'd still be working within my core passion, which was to protect and better the lives of all the world's people with clean energy. One might believe that I became an environmentalist because I love the Earth, but it would be much more accurate to say that I love people, and I want to protect the Earth because people live on it.

I'd worked for Greenpeace as a campaign manager for almost a decade, and before that I'd directed Project Underground, an organization committed to protecting the human rights of people struggling with mining and oil operations. I came to realize that I could now effect more change as an entrepreneur. Not to be crass, but money talks—and while the world's governments might be able to ignore activism, they can't ignore the voice of commerce. The market won't be denied in this day and age, or at least that's the theory of the political economy with which we seem to be stuck.

The main question was, *What kind of business would I start?* I remembered when, 11 years earlier, I'd hiked up to a gas plant that British Petroleum had installed in Papua New Guinea's highlands and witnessed the ravages of Dirty Energy on that gorgeous land. I recalled turning my face to the sun and thinking that solar power was the remedy to the sickness, pollution, and corruption that ol' King CONG was spreading throughout the world. The Huli and Engans wanted electricity, but they could get it so much more easily from solar panels in their community than by letting the place be dug up for gas to be exported and returned to run turbines in some imaginary future called "development," or "devil-upment" as one of the country's wisest politicians called it. Remembering these experiences, I knew that harnessing solar power and making it available for universal need was the business I wanted to be in.

When I first met Alec Guettel in 1990, he was wearing a penguin suit and protesting outside the Montréal protocol negotiations in London. I was 19 and attending these meetings as a youth delegate of the Australian government. We were the good guys trying to control ozone-depleting substances, whereas the United States and the United Kingdom, with their respective vested interests in DuPont and Imperial Chemical Industries—major producers of chlorofluorocarbons and other ozone-depleting substances—were, in our eyes, not such good characters. Alec was there with a group of student activists protesting the United States' performance in these talks, and as a like mind I stepped outside the convention hall while Margaret Thatcher was speaking and went to have a beer with Alec and some other activists, or "ratbags," as they were called by some of the delegates inside.

The rest is history: we became firm friends.

Around 2001 we first talked of the need for clever, clean-energy companies, but it really wasn't until 2006 that our conversation grew serious. Prior to that, around 2004, I remember flying to New York to attend a UN Commission on Sustainable Development meeting about global warming and crashing on his couch for a couple of days. We stayed up late one night, drinking at some bar in SoHo like the lads we once were and discussing the idea of putting solar panels on the California State Water Project.

I'd worked in California a couple of years before and had become obsessed with the aqueduct that runs through and irrigates the Central Valley. It's the Golden State's largest single consumer of electricity, with 12 pumping stations along its route. Its course—from Sacramento down through Fresno to Bakersfield and beyond—means that plenty of sunlight falls on it. Alec said then that he would bankroll me to make the business idea happen and support me with his networks and know-how. "You're crazy," I said. I knew how to use the "vampire effect" to hurt companies that are doing the wrong thing—that is, to destroy them by shining a light on them—but I didn't know much about building a company.

But then, as I went on to run Greenpeace's political work in Australia and the Pacific for five years, I realized that I had at least some of what it takes to run a startup. For a start, working in a nonprofit environment teaches you how to do a lot with a little. Greenpeace may be well known globally, but resources are always scarce. Even though we had a 100-person staff in five offices in the region, we had a lot of work to do—stopping activities such as illegal logging, pirate fishing, and toxic dumping. Aligning the team to common objectives was key to working there, and it's how you have to think when planning a startup.

But it wasn't until I read American community activist Bill Moyers's book *Doing Democracy* that I really understood how an entrepreneur could bring about social change. Moyers explains the eight stages that all social movements go through and the four roles that are required to push them through these stages, including that of small businesses as change agents. At points in any struggle to solve a social problem, Moyers says, you have to demonstrate that there's an alternative to business as usual—especially once you've convinced the majority of people that the current authorities don't have the solutions.

In 2006 Alec and I became determined to build a business that would demonstrate the scaled solution of solar electricity for the masses. Coincidentally, serving the end users was a great profit focus because while the industry had been growing like gangbusters in the preceding 10 years, that growth had been primarily in the area of hardware, so we saw a huge opportunity in the customer-facing sales space. Many industries have had a period of growth predominantly focused on hardware, driven by engineers and technologists, only to watch their margins taken by companies downstream that served the end user. Dell and Apple come to mind—two companies that sold not only hardware but also a service to their customers.

So as we looked at the solar industry as an opportunity, we wanted to start a business providing consumers with the best possible proposition in terms of price, product, and brand. As we brainstormed different business models, we focused on delivering a combination of good energy and great service. We looked at everything from solar-powered coolers for tailgate parties to a residential solar sales company, but it wasn't until we teamed up with Andrew "Birchy" Birch that we really nailed down the future of Sungevity because he had the acumen to really make it happen.

Forming the Sungevity Team

I'd met Birchy through an academic friend at the University of New South Wales, which has one of the most prestigious electrical-engineering schools in the world due to its good work around the policy and the economics of the Solar Ascent. My friend introduced Birchy as a crazy Scottish banker who was doing an electrical-engineering master's degree with a focus on economics, and who, despite his banking background, was doing fine with the physics.

After Birchy graduated from the University of New South Wales, BP snapped him up to be a Big Business development exec in its solar division. There he encouraged the company—which at the time was one of the top three manufacturers of solar panels in the world—to think outside the Big Oil box and focus more on the customer's needs as an end user of BP's solar-panel product. He encouraged the company to use its substantial capital to create good customer finance solutions for solar systems on homes and also to use its distribution network and household name to market and sell solar products. He felt this would be the best way for the company to make its 20-year-old solar division profitable in a period during which manufacturing was being scaled by other companies better suited to the task.

Instead BP dug more holes in the ground because when you have a hammer, everything starts looking like a nail. In BP's case, this myopia manifested itself in the company's decision to open new mines to produce silicon for new factories to turn the silicon into cells, albeit through a global supply chain. As a result of these choices, BP Solar slipped from being one of the world's top solar companies at the start of the century to being a minor player by 2010, and BP Solar closed its doors permanently at the end of 2011 because of its inability to compete in an oversupplied market. (Solyndra wasn't the only casualty of low-cost, affordable solar panels.) By then Birchy had left BP to join Sungevity, and I'd bet there are some people at BP who wish they'd listened to him then, before they spent several hundred million dollars barking up the wrong tree.

So by 2008 Birchy had built us a business plan to realize my and Alec's dream of creating solar energy for universal need. His father is a longtime chef and hotelier, so Birchy also brought to our business his dad's work ethic and customer service expertise. The biggest insight Birchy had was that we could use the Internet to change the way solar was sold. It turned out that Birchy, like me, had been reading a lot about Dell, and it was clear to us that what Dell had done with the bundle of components we now know as the personal computer was what we needed to do with a solar system.

Leveraging the Power of the Internet

Before Dell and other companies, such as Apple and Gateway, brought retail savvy and user orientation to the table, the personal-computer industry was a dog's breakfast—a mess. As you may recall, we would go into a store somewhere downtown or in a mall, and a man in a white lab coat would ask us questions that we didn't understand but were too embarrassed to push back on, like "Do you want a 286 motherboard or a 24-bit modem?" I for one didn't know what I wanted, but I'd somehow get led through a process to buy "a box," as they were called, which I took home at great expense, unclear whether or not it would serve my needs.

Now we buy computers online, knowing they will be shipped to us and that they'll work—straight out of the box—far better than we could have imagined just a decade ago. Birchy's long-term business plan was to make our company's customer experience as seamless as Dell's in the way we served solar electricity to suburbia. He envisioned an online, interactive quote and monitoring solution for installed systems to interface with the customer. This is what we now have come to call the iQuote and OurSungevity.

When we were conceptualizing how Sungevity would work, the fledgling solar industry felt a lot like the way the PC industry did in its early days. As Birchy pointed out, a typical conversation between a solar provider and a potential customer was ugly:

> "Do you want a Fronius or a Kaco inverter?"
> "Um, I'm not sure what an inverter is."
> "You like 60-cell format or 72-cell format panels?"
> "Ack, I'm not sure."
> "Will 175 or 170 watt work for you?"
> [Helpless silence from the customer.]

If you looked at the websites of the solar companies in the space in 2006, you'd find a lot of clutter covering technical specifications of hardware. But average customers care less about this than what the hardware can deliver. All they really wanted was the service—electricity! This is the classic trap of young industries fixated on their own brilliance and trying to sell features, not benefits. Michael Dell famously disrupted (from his dorm room) all those clunky corner-store experiences in the early personal-computer days with a simple website that let you easily select your choices for a PC; his company then configured the machine to do what you wanted and shipped it to you.

By the time we were launching Sungevity, Dell's innovative solution—using the Internet to deliver superior service—had spread. Take, for example, what Expedia has done for the travel business, or Amazon for book selling, or Zappos for shoes. But this sort of innovation had not been applied to the construction industry, specifically the solar construction projects that we wanted to see spread across suburbia to slow the pace of climate change by creating a greater supply of clean energy. So the question was, *How do you apply the tools of the Internet to the sale of solar solutions for homes in America?* Birchy, Alec, and I had a few good ideas, and more came as our team grew and we consulted potential customers and other partners in the solar space.

I asked Alec whether he thought I needed a master's degree in business administration (MBA), and he said no. "Read a lot" was his suggestion. The only real benefit of getting an MBA, he told me, was the little black book that you get out of it; but as a result of my long career in activism, my work organizing campaigns, and the people I'd met along the way, I already had one. And one of the first people we recruited, initially by using her backyard shack as an office and then by slowly sucking her in as our first employee, was an old friend, Martha Belcher. She has an MBA and the operational prowess to set up the processes and procedures for our business, and I knew she'd become the systems queen we needed to deliver an excellent customer experience. That was enough, he said.

Plus we had Alec's big black book. Sure enough, it *was* enough: his friends and family, as well as some of mine and Birchy's, composed a big enough network to capitalize our business and allow us to start our plan of building the Apple of residential solar.

Our early investors took a gamble on a vision of solar for universal need (which I call SFUN) and our sense of how we could get there, or at least how we might find the path toward it. With their help we've created a business that's truly remarkable.

As we built the company, Alec kept us honest and on track with five icons that symbolized the qualities we had to display to succeed: a tennis net, a target, a roller coaster, a handshake, and a magnet.

The tennis net reminds us that the ball is always in our court; it's always our move. We shouldn't wait for someone else to act or reply; rather, we have to make things happen. I believe this bias toward action is the great hallmark of entrepreneurs, activists, and anybody who wants to get things done.

The target is a bit more obvious; it means "stay focused." I had always felt as a campaign manager at nonprofits that focus was the greatest resource we had, for if we could avoid distractions and home in on the target, we could achieve great results. Avoiding "ideaphoria" is evergreen advice.

The roller-coaster ride was to warn us, as we aimed to be successful businesspeople, that reaching our goal was going to involve lots of twists and turns, gut-wrenching falls, moments of scream-inducing terror, the desire to vomit, and the sense that the thing could come off the rails at any time—sensations that are followed by sheer joy and relief. How apt this icon turned out to be; it's been a helluva ride!

The handshake symbolizes partnership, which is critical to success, especially for a company like ours—built by friends. Most businesses fail over the founding partnership. Partnering with other people is a skill that requires the use of one's ears and one's mouth in the ratio that they were given to us—that is, 2 to 1. As well as good listening skills, partnering requires emotional intelligence and maturity.

Finally, the magnet is about attracting talent. Whether your company is in startup mode or already profitable, you need to be engaging, attracting, and telling your company's story to get the best people to join the mission.

Breaking Down the Barriers to Solar

At Sungevity we created a plan to break down the three greatest barriers to the mass adoption of solar: cost, hassle, and mistrust. We've seen the cost come down because of the commoditization of the hardware components of the solar system. The panels are sold at a certain amount per watt to residential companies like ours (when we started in 2008 we were paying $4 per watt to suppliers, but now it's closer to $1 per watt). Businesses like Sungevity have made selling and installing solar for residential customers around the world more efficient. Our remote solar-design tool cuts 10 percent of the cost of making a sale because we don't have to drive to a dozen houses before making one. Equally important has been the introduction of third-party financing to cover this outlay. Solar leasing has been

the game changer in our industry (as discussed in chapter 4)—
and we're still looking at more-creative financial solutions.

Cost

Let's get into the nitty-gritty of how the solar lease works:
Customers have a solar system installed on the home at no
cost, and then every month they pay for the electricity that
they receive from the system. When their solar panels produce
more electricity than customers can use, that electricity goes
back into the grid to be used elsewhere, and it earns them credit
for electricity they may use later, such as at night. As we've discussed, this is a substantial money-saving proposition for most
customers in the states we serve.

The complex financial structure on the backside of this deal
is the most important innovation in the residential solar industry in the past decade. In short, an investor seeking tax credits
and depreciation values can monetize these by paying for the
system to be installed. This covers most of the cost to install,
and the remainder is paid off through lease payments over the
life of the system. This model has been so wildly successful that
it has gone from no market share just four years ago to being
the majority of the residential solar market in the United States
today. By the end of 2011, third-party-financed systems were
60 percent of the home solar market.

When you think about it, it makes sense that a solar-power
system should be financed just like all other energy systems
are. In that familiar model, you have a contract with the utility provider and you make a monthly payment, which is used
to offset the cost of building the power plant that generates the
electricity. There is a cost of capital, or the rent that some finan-
cier is extracting for lending the power company the money to

build the power plant, included in this price you pay. So it is now with solar.

Hassle

On to the hassle that customers expect when considering a solar option for their homes. What Sungevity is doing with its iQuote is a game changer of a different kind that makes going solar easy. With it we can effectively calculate the electricity-producing potential of the home wherever sufficient aerial or satellite photographs exist, which is now much of the world. As solar panels become more widely accepted and their production increases, they'll be integrated into buildings' facades—the windows as well as the roof. With our software tool, we can determine what a building's output would be if it were covered with solar panels, which is an important step in marketing and financing that solar-system installation.

We look forward to a bright future because our market will grow from thousands of units to millions of units in a few short years using this tool. And there are many more tools in the toolkit that our New Greatest Generation can build to ensure the Solar Ascent. This is where many hot jobs will originate in the years to come. Software solutions to help solar scale will have a big business impact with a lot less resource requirement than some parts of the advanced-energy economy we've discussed.

Trust

At Sungevity we're also focusing on some of the tools needed to break down the barrier of mistrust, specifically social networking and peer pride. For example, we have a social iQuote, which helps feed the virality of the solar experience so that it can spread through neighborhoods quickly.

Shortly after starting Sungevity, we realized the significance of virality in spreading the benefits of solar, and now with our social Sunshine Network software, we're trying to feed it. We're building web products such as an online referral center to help our Rooftop Revolutionary customers get others to sign on to the Solar Ascent. We've made it a bit like a game, and you get financial as well as social rewards for telling your friends to go solar and spreading the savings and the sunshine of the Sungevity solar lease. I don't want to dwell too long on our model lest I bore you, but most of our business comes from this sort of online word of mouth. And with third-party partners like the home improvement giant Lowe's and the environmental group the Sierra Club recommending us to people who know and trust them, we're trying to make solar something that everyone not only feels confident in but also believes is cool to have.

It all sounds so easy when I say it now, but of course creating an entirely new process for selling solar and harnessing the value of leasing for our customers did not just fall into place without some trouble. And at the time of this writing, managing the cash flow and the operational processes of our phenomenal growth and keeping our customers satisfied are still challenges. We actually launched our business at the start of 2008, at the beginning of the Great Recession. I laugh now thinking about it—how insane we were to do something entirely new and different just as the world's financial system started to fall apart. I think that in some ways beginning a business at the time of the Great Recession made our company stronger, and surviving as we have until now suggests that our model works and will really succeed as the economy recovers.

Birchy pushed us to keep dreaming big, and we broke down the conventional solar sales cycle to 16 steps—quoting, selling, permitting, installing, inspecting, interconnecting, and so on—which we sought to standardize and digitize in our business platform.

With the couple million dollars we raised from investors, we set out to hire the software developers required to build our dream business. We put a request for proposals on Internet job boards for software engineers and dot-com survivors around the world. We received bids from everywhere—from Bulgaria to Bangalore to the Bay Area—but the best bid actually came from a company called Extro down the road from where I used to work in Sydney. There were a couple of tough choices at the end of a $0.5 million tender process between Extro and another developer, but Birchy's wife, Lulu—who was living with all of this day in and day out—made the call. She was right!

In a few short months, this twentysomething, Adam Pryor, and his team of a half dozen code writers made history. They had created the tool for remote solar design, which allows us to calculate the electricity-generating potential of any building, and integrated it into a complete customer relationship management database for all of the stages of the solar sale. The avoided truck rolls alone save a lot of carbon pollution as we sell millions of systems, but more important is how this platform makes going solar so easy. Extro blew our minds by being on time and under budget; and with the product they created, we launched Sungevity in 2008.

We then went on to win numerous awards for our software ingenuity, including the Public Broadcasting Service Innovator of the Year award for moving the planet forward in 2011, in a field that included Serious Materials and other great companies. But perhaps the greatest accolade came when we showed some of the algorithms and code to a Microsoft worker who wanted to understand how we were using the aerial image feeds his company had licensed to us to build a three-dimensional model of a home. Once he got the complex math and clever design of the software, he whistled and said that out of Microsoft's 300 developers working with these photo datasets, none of them had been able to do what we'd done.

We have now refined that tool and built it out in many ways, and the reason for this story is not to brag about our intellectual property but rather to show what some creative thinking and great talent can do to advance the Solar Ascent. We have broken the mold for how solar is sold, making it much less likely that you'll have a guy come knocking on your door to take measurements and draw up plans. This has significant cost-saving implications for the entire industry, and it just makes for a better customer experience.

This efficiency and creativity is what we need to achieve the potential of our Next Great Generation. This shift will make customers more likely to refer us to others, creating a ball of sunshine that grows from neighbor to neighbor across communities around the world; and serving all these customers will require more ingenious entrepreneurs to build software solutions that can work with ours to spread sunshine online. We look forward to the competition!

By the end of 2011, Sungevity was more than 200 people strong. Our offices in Oakland's Jack London Square are cool and cavernous, and every day in our airy environment I feel the buzz of passion, imagination, and commitment that our free-range staff brings to Sungevity's mission.

Another of the many rock stars who have become engaged by our vision is Patrick Crane, who was previously the chief marketing officer of LinkedIn. Patrick helped build that business, which has disrupted the recruiting and human resources industries by getting new signups for the social network to a pace of one per second at the time he left in 2010. We'll need that kind of velocity to administer the installation of solar systems on enough roofs to ensure the necessary change from dirty to clean energy in the twenty-first century. We believe that the total addressable market is maybe 50 million roofs, and mathematically we can get to that many only with a much more efficient customer acquisition and sales cycle and a much cleaner fulfillment process than currently exists.

Patrick helped articulate Sungevity's mission "to build the world's most energized network of people who power their lives with sunshine." We'd always known the SFUN vision and how we want to create a constituency for the change to an advanced-energy economy, but naming it and claiming the network effect as the means to get there give us a chance to get to those 50 million roofs. Taking solar adoption online and harnessing solar enthusiasm as a social network phenomenon is the best way to achieve solar for universal need.

Overall our contribution to the Solar Ascent is triggering a Rooftop Revolution around the globe as people become liberated from Dirty Energy, building an ever-growing group of citizens touched by the benefits of going solar. Those people then become a motivating force for the political changes needed for other solar businesses to deliver solutions more broadly.

Shine the Light!

I hope in this saga you see ways you can contribute as a solar citizen or solar entrepreneur. We need these roles more than anything. Recently, I came across a definition of *entrepreneurship* on Inc.com: "the pursuit of opportunity without regard to resources currently controlled." I think that nails it, and I also figure it explains why activists make great entrepreneurs. If you've ever organized against all odds to stop some large government or corporate interest from building a block of apartments or an incinerator, or if you've sought to change your Constitution the way Australian Republicans are still trying to separate their country from the British Monarchy (yep, the land of my youth is still trying to catch up with revolutionary America in this basic regard), you know what it's like to do a lot with a little against formidable inertia. Indeed you almost have to *disregard* resources currently controlled because if you focus on that, you may decide not to pursue your goals at all.

Yet activists prevail. Social movements make history, not just powerful white men and corporations. And entrepreneurs build big, popular markets. Margaret Mead, quoted at the beginning of this epilogue and referenced frequently at political campfire discussions and social-change training centers in my youth, had it mostly right: small groups of thoughtful and committed citizens do change the world—but only by bringing in lots more folks to their cause. The hows and the why-fors of these movements are sometimes less easy to follow, but in the significant civilizational change that we're on the cusp of by "going solar," the few and the brave who do it now will change not only the power systems but also the power relations that dominate our society.

"Get a job, you bum."

I still hear these words inside my head. And I still laugh. As president of a multimillion-dollar enterprise, I work in a role these hecklers might approve of. It's probably the only time I've ever done what they've asked of me.

What You Can Do as a Rooftop Revolutionary

▶ Experience the ease and the affordability of going solar by getting a solar iQuote at www.sungevity.com.

▶ Follow Sungevity on Twitter (@sungevity), Facebook (facebook .com/sungevity), and LinkedIn (linkedin.com/company/ Sungevity). Follow Danny Kennedy on Twitter (@dannyksfun).

▶ If you're not a homeowner, invest in a community solar project at Solar Mosaic (www.solarmosaic.com).

▶ Share this book and shine a light on the Solar Ascent for someone who is skeptical.

Notes

Chapter 1: Sunny Side Up

The world loves Apple products, and Wall Street loves the company, which in 2012 surpassed Exxon as the most valuable in the world.

"Apple Passes Exxon as Most Valuable US Company in Terms of Market Cap," *Huffington Post,* January 25, 2012, http://www.huffingtonpost.com/2012/01/25/apple-passes-exxon-market-cap_n_1231074.html (accessed March 12, 2012).

More column inches were devoted to the Solyndra story in most outlets than to Japan's Fukushima nuclear-power-plant disaster, which wrote down the Tokyo Electric Power Company's value by $13 billion and required a $9 billion bailout by the people of Japan.

Kentaro Hamada and Linda Sieg, "Japan's Stricken Nuclear Operator Set for $13 Billion Bailout," *Reuters,* January 26, 2012, http://www.reuters.com/article/2012/01/26/us-tepco-idUSTRE80P04B20120126 (accessed March 12, 2012).

In 2012 oil barons such as the Koch brothers will spend many millions on TV ad campaigns to tar President Barack Obama with the same brush they used on Solyndra.

Justin Sink, "Koch-Backed Group Spends $6 Million on Anti-Obama Solyndra Ad," *The Hill,* January 16, 2012, http://thehill.com/video/campaign/204357-koch-backed-group-spends-6-million-on-anti-obama-solyndra-ad (accessed March 12, 2012).

Those who have the most to lose, the opponents of solar, will come out with fists flying—as the US Chamber of Commerce did in the 2010 election cycle. The massive business lobby outspent the Republican and Democratic National Committees combined to further its official policy of digging up every last ounce of fuel in the ground and burning it as soon as possible.

Bill McKibben, "Burning America's Future," *Los Angeles Times,* January 18, 2012, http://www.latimes.com/news/opinion/la-oe-mckibben-a-spectacularly-bad-idea-for-energy-20120118,0,2539447.story?track=rss (accessed March 12, 2012).

And public opinion is clear: according to the SCHOTT Solar Barometer, when voters were asked to select an energy source they would financially support if they were in charge of US energy policy, 39 percent said they would choose solar power while a measly 3 percent chose coal—almost the inverse ratio of our representatives in Congress.

"New Poll: 9 out of 10 Americans Support Solar, Across Political Spectrum," Solar Energy Industries Association, November 1, 2011, http://www.seia.org/cs/news_detail?pressrelease.id=1710 (accessed March 12, 2012).

Greenpeace, the environmental advocacy organization, released a parody video that exposed the reality that the API campaign wasn't divulging—that these energy sources are damaging and unsustainable and that the jobs the corporations claim to create are only temporary.

James Gerken, "'I Vote 4 Energy' Video Spoofs American Petroleum Institute Ad Campaign," *Huffington Post,* January 6, 2012, http://www.huffingtonpost.com/2012/01/05/i-vote-4-energy-video-spoof-api_n_1186400.html (accessed March 12, 2012).

As the API's spokesman said when launching Vote 4 Energy, "It's not about candidates, it's not about political parties, it's not even about political philosophy. Energy should not be a partisan issue. . . . We believe a vote for energy will elevate the energy conversation."

Mark Green, "Starting the Energy Debate," *EnergyTomorrow Blog,* January 5, 2012, http://energytomorrow.org/blog/starting-the-energy-debate/#/type/all (accessed March 12, 2012).

US solar-generated electricity expanded in 2011 by 45 percent over the first three quarters of 2010.

US Solar Market Insight, 1st Quarter 2011, Solar Energy Industries Association and GTM Research, www.seia.org/galleries/pdf/SMI-Q1-2011-ES.pdf (accessed March 12, 2012).

In comparison, natural-gas electrical generation rose only 1.6 percent, while nuclear output declined by 2.8 percent and coal-generated electricity dropped by 4.2 percent.

"Renewables Now Provide 12 Percent of Domestic Energy," *Clean Edge News,* January 5, 2012, http://cleanedge.com/resources/news/Renewables-Now-Provide-12-Percent-of-Domestic-Energy-Up-14-Percent (accessed March 12, 2012).

In 2010, 16 states installed more than enough to supply approximately 2,000 homes, compared with only four states in 2007.

US Solar Market Insight, 1st Quarter 2011, Solar Energy Industries Association and GTM Research, http://www.seia.org/galleries/pdf/SMI-Q1-2011-ES.pdf (accessed March 12, 2012).

China enjoyed such a burst of solar power that it recalibrated the target in its twelfth five-year plan to 15 gigawatts installed by 2015—50 percent higher than the previous target and 50 percent more than we expect to have in the United States.

"China Releases Solar Industry 5-Year Plan," *Green Growth Investment*, February 25, 2012, http://greengrowthinvestment.com/china-releases-solar -industry-5-year-plan (accessed March 12, 2012).

On the subcontinent, Pakistan has passed the point where solar power is cheaper than a lot of electricity that comes from diesel generators, and India is upping its target from 20 to 33 gigawatts to be installed by 2020.

"India Solar Compass," January 2012 ed., *Bridge to India*, http://bridgetoindia .com/reports (accessed March 12, 2012).

Germany produced more than 18 billion kilowatt-hours of solar electricity in 2011. That's 60 percent more than it produced the year before and is enough to supply 5 million households for a year.

"Germany Generates 60% More Solar Electricity in 2011," *Energy Matters*, January 2, 2012, http://www.energymatters.com.au/index.php?main_ page=news_article&article_id=1960 (accessed March 12, 2012).

All the others, including natural gas, are going up in price—no matter what the gas industry says. Although there is *currently* a surplus of natural gas in the US market due to the lower cost of fracking, it won't last because when you're dealing with a finite energy source and consuming it in the vast amounts that Americans do, it's impossible to keep costs low over the long term.

"Why the Solar Industry Lacks Pricing Power," PowerFin Partners, December 20, 2011, http://www.powerfinpartners.com/new_site/pdf/Why%20 the%20Solar%20Industry%20Lacks%20Pricing%20Power%20122011.pdf (accessed March 12, 2012).

Globally, solar is the fastest-growing industry, valued at more than $100 billion. And in the United States, it's the fastest-growing job-creating sector. Solar grew nearly 7 percent as an employment generator while the economy flatlined—a tenth of that growth from August 2010 to 2011.

Paul Krugman, "Here Comes the Sun," *New York Times*, November 6, 2011, http://www.nytimes.com/2011/11/07/opinion/krugman-here-comes-solar -energy.html?_r=1&hp (accessed March 12, 2012).

Just before Christmas 2011, Google invested $94 million in four large-scale solar photovoltaic projects, edging the total amount the search giant invested in clean-energy projects toward $900 million.

"Google Shines on Solar Sector with $94m Investment," *BusinessGreen*, December 21, 2011, http://www.businessgreen.com/bg/news/2133967/google -shines-solar-sector-usd94m-investment?WT.rss_f=Home&WT.rss_

a=Google+shines+on+solar+sector+with+$94m+investment (accessed March 12, 2012).

Not to be beaten, and always one to place a bet when assets are artificially depressed, investment guru Warren Buffett dropped almost $2 billion on California's Topaz Solar Farm, which will sell solar electricity to Pacific Gas and Electric (PG&E), the local utility company, and generate electricity for about 160,000 homes.

Julianne Pepitone, "Warren Buffett's MidAmerican Buys First Solar Plant," *CNNMoney,* December 7, 2011, http://money.cnn.com/2011/12/07/technology/ buffett_first_solar/index.htm (accessed March 12, 2012).

Indeed Bloomberg New Energy Finance recorded the trillionth dollar of investment in clean energy since its records started in 2004.

Nathaniel Bullard, "$1 Trillion Speaks Louder Than UN Talks," *Bloomberg,* December 7, 2011, http://www.bloomberg.com/news/2011-12-07/-1-trillion -speaks-louder-than-un-talks.html (accessed March 12, 2012).

Germany now gets a whopping 20 percent of its power from clean, sustainable energy, including solar power, and the country has become a laboratory for the kind of electricity supply that the world will benefit from in years to come.

"Crossing the 20 Percent Mark: Green Energy Use Jumps in Germany," *Spiegel Online International,* August 30, 2011, http://www.spiegel.de/ international/0,1518,783314,00.html (accessed March 12, 2012).

The rest of Europe didn't want the Germans to hog the solar spotlight, and now many other places have at times adopted a higher density of clean electricity in their grid than even Germany—such as Denmark (more than 30 percent), Spain (35 percent), and Portugal (50 percent).

Derived from http://www.iea.org/stats/electricitydata.asp?COUNTRY_ CODE=DK (2009); http://en.wikipedia.org/wiki/Renewable_energy_ in_the_European_Union#Portugal; and http://en.wikipedia.org/wiki/ Renewable_energy_in_the_European_Union#Spain (last modified February 16, 2012; accessed March 12, 2012).

In Crimea, Ukraine, a Vienna-based developer, Activ Solar, built the world's largest solar park, a project of more than 100 megawatts in capacity—one-tenth the size of a nuke—and worth about 300 million euros (US $387 million), according to reports.

Mark Roca, "Europe's Biggest Solar Park Completed with Russian Bank Debt," *Energy News World,* December 29, 2011, http://energynewsworld.wordpress .com/2011/12/29/europes-biggest-solar-park-completed-with-russian-bank -debt (accessed March 12, 2012).

In spite of the staggering advances Germany has made, politics is besieging it. The country is experiencing a backlash against renewable energy, led by fiscal conservatives in the German parliament who believe that the incentives for solar power will cost too much in the future.

"Solar Energy Row Is an 'Undignified Spectacle,'" *Spiegel Online International,* January 20, 2012, http://www.spiegel.de/international/ger many/0,1518,810370,00.html (accessed March 12, 2012).

More importantly, 50 percent of Germany's solar panels are owned by individuals and farms, not big corporate generators. As one writer put it, this is a good thing: "Decentralized power generation, more relocalization and reregionalization of economic activity, the world getting smaller while more connected and therefore in a way bigger at the same time."

Mat McDermott, "Over Half of Germany's Renewable Energy Owned by Citizens and Farmers, Not Utility Companies," *TreeHugger,* January 6, 2012, http://www.treehugger.com/renewable-energy/over-half -germany-renewable-energy-owned-citizens-not-utility-companies.html (accessed March 12, 2012).

The year 2011 marked the first time in history that these powerhouses invested more money in renewable energy than in fossil fuels.

"Renewable Power Trumps Fossil Fuels for First Time," *Los Angeles Times/ Bloomberg,* November 25, 2011, http://articles.latimes.com/2011/nov/25/ business/la-fi-renewables-20111125 (accessed March 12, 2012).

Every state is different, but the economics are improving all the time, and by 2015, according to projections by the Department of Energy, two-thirds of American households will save money by using solar electricity.

Paul Denham, Robert M. Margolis, Sean Ong, and Billy Roberts, "Break-Even Cost for Residential Photovoltaics in the United States: Key Drivers and Sensitivities," National Renewable Energy Laboratory, December 2009, http:// www.nrel.gov/docs/fy10osti/46909.pdf (accessed March 12, 2012).

The investments made in solar-product manufacturing by China, Korea, India, Germany, the United States, and other countries over the past five years have broadly tripled the production capacity, bringing down the end-product price more than 50 percent.

"Module Pricing," *Solarbuzz,* March 2012, http://www.solarbuzz.com/ node/3184 (accessed March 12, 2012).

Meanwhile, the fossil-fuel electricity-generation industries shed 2 percent of their employees.

It is our conclusion from http://www.economicmodeling.com (accessed March 12, 2012) that fossil-fuel electric power generation (NAICS 221112) lost

1,614 jobs, or –2 percent; this does not include distribution, just generation (http://www.census.gov/econ/industry/current/c221112.htm); electric power distribution (NAICS 221122) lost 2,279 jobs, or –1 percent (http://www.census .gov/econ/industry/current/c221122.htm); and electric power transmission, control, and distribution (NAICS 22112) was flat (0 percent), with only 39 jobs added (http://www.census.gov/econ/industry/current/c22112.htm).

The conservative intergovernmental International Energy Agency (IEA) is now predicting that by 2050 most of the world's electricity could come from solar power.

Cédric Philibert, "Solar Energy Perspectives," International Energy Agency World Solar Congress, September 1, 2011, http://www.iea.org/speech/2011/ solar_perspectives.pdf (accessed March 12, 2012).

A study by the Institute for Local Self-Reliance showed that making the United States a 100 percent solar nation would create nearly 10 million jobs.

"Energy Self-Reliant States," 2nd ed., Institute for Local Self-Reliance, May 2011, downloadable at http://energyselfreliantstates.org/reports; also summarized at http://www.energyselfreliantstates.org/content/local-solar -could-power-mountain-west-2011-all-america-2026 (accessed March 12, 2012).

Chapter 2: Empires of the Sun *Dirty Energy's Petty Politics*

When one of Reagan's people was asked why, the spokesperson responded that solar panels were "not a technology befitting a superpower."

John Wihbey, "Jimmy Carter's Solar Panels: A Lost History That Haunts Today," *Yale Forum on Climate Change and the Media*, November 11, 2008, http://www.yaleclimatemediaforum.org/2008/11/jimmy-carters-solar-panels (accessed March 12, 2012).

But get this: the administration of George W. Bush—a staunch Republican, like his hero Reagan—put solar *back* on the White House.

Lise, "Solar Panels at the White House," *CoolerPlanet.com*, March 8, 2008, http://blog.coolerplanet.com/2008/03/08/solar-panels-at-the-white-house (accessed March 12, 2012).

Right now, as *Grist* writer Dave Roberts put it, "Republicans who stray, who say anything accommodating, who even acknowledge that scientists might be on to something are savaged by the base and the conservative media complex."

David Roberts, "A Few Brave Conservatives Speak Up for Climate Sanity," *Grist*, June 16, 2011, http://climatechangepsychology.blogspot.com/2011/06/ david-roberts-grist-few-brave.html (accessed March 12, 2012).

Look at Newt Gingrich, who in 2008 went from endorsing Al Gore's view of climate change to adopting a "Drill, baby, drill; dig, baby, dig" line through his nonprofit American Solutions for Winning the Future. He took $825,000 from the coal giant Peabody Energy and $500,000 from Devon Energy, an oil and gas player.

Dan Eggen, "Donations Flowed to Gingrich's Nonprofit after He Shifted on Energy Issues in 2008," *Washington Post*, December 28, 2011, http://www .washingtonpost.com/politics/donations-flowed-to-gingrichs-nonprofit -after-he-shifted-on-energy-issues-in-2008/2011/12/20/gIQA6PBKNP_story .html?wprss=rss_politics (accessed March 12, 2012).

In an op-ed on the politically influential blog *Politico.com*, Norquist and a colleague regurgitated some oft-made claims of the fossil-fuel lobby: that clean-energy requirements in some states were costing jobs and money, that legislators would be wise to repeal laws that require some amount of clean energy in their electricity system to level the playing field (as though pitting nascent clean energy technologies against the behemoths of the fossil-fuel industry would be a fair match), and that subsidies for the renewable-power industry are a waste.

Grover G. Norquist and Patrick Gleason, "Rethink Renewable Energy Mandates," *The Hill*, December 18, 2011, http://www.politico.com/news/ stories/1211/70610.html (accessed March 12, 2012).

For example, in Colorado the RPS requirements to meet 20 percent of electricity needs by 2020 will be achieved eight years in advance, that is, in 2012, and will save customers $100 million in electricity costs while creating thousands of jobs and substantial tax benefits.

"Colorado to Achieve 30% Renewables 8 Years Early, Saves Ratepayers Big Bucks," VoteSolar, November 13, 2011, http://votesolar.org/2011/11/colorado -to-achieve-30-renewables-8-years-early-ratepayer-savings-of-409-million (accessed March 12, 2012).

On the other side of the ledger, coal costs more than it creates in value, according to a 2011 study in the *American Economic Review*, which estimates that in the United States coal creates roughly $53 billion in damages per year—a cost that is more than twice as high as the market price of the electricity.

Nicholas Z. Muller, Robert Mendelsohn, and William Nordhaus, "Environmental Accounting for Pollution in the United States Economy," *American Economic Review* 101 (5) (August 2011) 1649–75, http://www.aeaweb.org/ articles.php?doi=10.1257/aer.101.5.1649 (accessed March 12, 2012).

Investing in the energy technology that will power the world is a good risk to take (all entrepreneurs in every new field take these risks), but do note: in Solyndra's case, its loan-guarantee program was set by the Bush administration,

so the investment in the company (and by extension the industry) wasn't an Obama or liberal interest, as some in the media would have you believe.

David Plouffe, "Did the Program That Funded the Solyndra Loan Start under George W. Bush? David Plouffe Says So," *Tampa Bay Times/PolitiFact.com,* October 30, 2011, http://www.politifact.com/truth-o-meter/statements/2011/nov/17/david-plouffe/solyndra-loan-george-w-bush-david-plouffe (accessed March 12, 2012).

Overall the clean-energy loan-guarantee program has had a higher than 90 percent success rate.

"Solyndra Accounts for Less Than 2% of the DOE's Successful Loan Program," *Daily Kos,* November 21, 2011, http://www.dailykos.com/story/2011/11/21/1038907/-Solyndra-accounts-for-less-than-2-of-the-DOE-s-successful-Loan-Program (accessed March 12, 2012).

In 1992, for example, I was at the United Nations (UN) meeting in New York where, after much deliberation and many months of late-night sessions, world leaders drafted the United Nations Framework Convention on Climate Change, a global effort to slow global warming.

"Background on the UNFCCC: The International Response to Climate Change," United Nations Framework Convention on Climate Change, http://unfccc.int/essential_background/items/6031.php (accessed March 12, 2012).

But young attendees, including yours truly (I was there as a journalist and youth activist), began to smell a rat in the framework when George H. W. Bush sent a message to the UN that "the American way of life was not up for negotiation"—meaning that Americans weren't going to stop using fossil fuels to create electricity or give up their SUVs.

Lee-Anne Broadhead, *International Environmental Politics: The Limits of Green Diplomacy* (Boulder, CO: Lynne Reinner, 2002), 51.

In another example of Dirty Energy foisting continued fossil dependence on a community and the community fighting back, just a year earlier the utility PG&E spent $50 million on a campaign to stop a local clean-energy initiative in Marin County.

Paul Hogarth, "Despite Spending $50 Million, California Rejects PG&E," *California Progress Report,* June 9, 2010, http://turn.org/article.php?id=1320 (accessed March 12, 2012).

Polling consistently shows that normal people across America like this idea: clean power of the people, by the people, for the people.

"Survey: Congress, White House Focus on Fossil Fuels, Nuclear Power Is out of Touch with Views of Mainstream America," Civil Society Institute,

November 3, 2011, http://www.civilsocietyinstitute.org/Media/110311release.
Cfm (accessed March 12, 2012).

In October 2011 a poll from the University of Texas at Austin showed that out of more than 3,400 consumers surveyed, 84 percent were worried about US consumption of oil from foreign sources and 76 percent about a lack of progress in finding better ways to use energy efficiently and develop renewable sources.

"Poll: Americans Believe US Headed in Wrong Direction on Energy," *University of Texas at Austin Newsroom*, October 9, 2011, http://www.utenergypoll.utexas.edu/newsroom (accessed March 12, 2012).

Chapter 3: Role Models for the Rooftop Revolution

In 1995 Ken was tried for a murder he couldn't have committed and was convicted in a Nigerian kangaroo court and then executed—all at the behest of Big Oil by his country's dictatorship, an act for which the country was suspended from the Commonwealth.

"Nigeria Hangs Human Rights Activists," BBC, November 10, 1995, http://news.bbc.co.uk/onthisday/hi/dates/stories/november/10/newsid_2539000/2539561.stm (accessed March 12, 2012).

Ken's family sued Shell for ordering his death, and in 2009 Shell settled out of court for $15 million.

Ed Pilkington, "Shell Pays out $15.5m over Saro-Wiwa Killing," *The Guardian*, June 8, 2009, http://www.guardian.co.uk/world/2009/jun/08/nigeria-usa (accessed March 12, 2012).

In the Energy Experts blog at NationalJournal.com, Nasheed explained to an American audience why he put solar on the palace: "This is a beginning step on the road to making the Maldives completely carbon-neutral by 2020."

Tom Madigan, "What Can the US Do to Cut Carbon?" October 12, 2010, http://energy.nationaljournal.com/2010/10/carbon-neutral-what-will-it-ta.php?comments=expandall#comments (accessed March 12, 2012).

Before beginning Solarcentury, Jeremy was the chief scientist for Greenpeace International and one of the key influencers of the Kyoto Protocol, an international agreement under the UN Framework Convention on Climate Change that bound 37 countries to reduce greenhouse-gas emissions.

"Kyoto Protocol to the United Nations Framework Convention on Climate Change," adopted May 9, 1992, United Nations Framework Convention on Climate Change, http://unfccc.int/essential_background/kyoto_protocol/items/1678.php (accessed March 12, 2012).

Forbes reported that the first major market GE's brand-new solar division is going to step into will be solar farms around wind turbines, which the company is also going to build and finance.

> Todd Woody, "GE, BrightSource and Sungevity Announce New Solar Projects as Solyndra Circus Continues," *Forbes*, October 14, 2011, http://www.forbes .com/sites/toddwoody/2011/10/14/ge-brightsource-and-sungevity-announce -new-solar-projects-as-solyndra-circus-continues (accessed March 12, 2012).

Hawaii gets more than 90 percent of its electricity from the burning of this oil product, which is why its electricity is extraordinarily expensive by US standards.

> "Average Electric Rates for Hawaiian Electric Co., Maui Electric Co. and Hawaii Electric Light Co.," Hawaiian Electric Company, http://www.heco .com/portal/site/heco/menuitem.508576f78baa14340b4c0610c510b1ca/?vgne xtoid=692e5e658e0fc010VgnVCM1000008119fea9RCRD&vgnextchannel=1 0629349798b4110VgnVCM1000005c011bacRCRD&vgnextfmt=defau&vgne xtrefresh=1&level=0&ct=article (accessed March 12, 2012).

And when I say "good return" I mean it because the value of the electricity generated by a solar system is around 6 percent—certainly better than the 1 or 2 percent that you might earn with a CD or similar investment instrument.

> CD rates as February 29, 2012, nothing higher than 1.08%, http://cdrates .bankaholic.com (accessed March 12, 2012).

For those who don't know the history, the Navajo Nation has been the site of some of the largest strip-mining operations ever seen, mostly at the direction of Peabody Energy Corporation.

> "Black Mesa Peabody Coal controversy," *Wikipedia,* last modified May 6, 2011, http://en.wikipedia.org/wiki/Black_Mesa_Peabody_Coal_debate (accessed March 12, 2012).

Through a spirited campaign over many years, the community was able to stop this madness and dismantle the Mohave Power Station in Laughlin. (You can even watch the implosion of the smokestack on YouTube.)

> "Mohave Generating Station Implosion 3/11/11 Laughlin, NV," YouTube, http://www.youtube.com/watch?v=i6nWma2SIds (accessed March 12, 2012).

Another incredible case in point is the wonderfully named Eden Full, a young woman you can Google and see present a TED talk on YouTube.

> "TEDxYYC - Eden Full - 02/26/10," YouTube, http://www.youtube.com/ watch?v=-zRannws9-M (accessed March 12, 2012).

Chapter 4: Take a Walk on the Sunny Side

Sometimes King CONG is more blunt, such as the Koch brothers' "Solyndra = Failure" campaign ads and when ExxonMobil CEO Lee Raymond appeared on PBS's *Charlie Rose* show and simply stated, "Solar is not a viable replacement" for oil.

"An Hour with CEO of ExxonMobil Lee Raymond, *Charlie Rose*, November 8, 2005, http://www.charlierose.com/view/interview/663 (accessed March 12, 2012).

The truth is, a 1,000-square-mile area of solar panels would provide all of our country's electricity needs, which is less than 10 percent of the land used by the oil and gas industry today.

Derived from multiple sources: Ken Zweibel, James Mason, and Vasilis Fthenaki, "By 2050 Solar Power Could End US Dependence on Foreign Oil and Slash Greenhouse Gas Emissions," *Scientific American* (January 2008), http://www.solarplan.org/Research/Z-M-F_A%20Solar%20Grand%20Plan_Scientific%20American_January%202008.pdf; http://www.landartgenerator.org/blagi/wp-content/uploads/2009/08/AreaRequired1000.jpg (graphic); and "America's Solar Energy Potential," *AmericanEnergyIndependence.com*, http://www.americanenergyindependence.com/solarenergy.aspx (accessed March 12, 2012).

Take haughty Lord Christopher Monckton—the British politician and climate change denialist—who was caught on tape encouraging members of the Australian mining industry to create a Fox News–style media network and use it to further the mining agenda.

Graham Readfearn, "Monckton's Push for an Australia Fox News," *The Drum*, February 2, 2012, http://www.abc.net.au/unleashed/3807130.html (accessed March 12, 2012).

The congressionally commissioned report that exposed this outrageous waste of taxpayer money was released the same week Solyndra shut down operations.

"Report to Congress on Contracting Fraud," Department of Defense, January 2011, http://www.sanders.senate.gov/graphics/Defense_Fraud_Report1.pdf (accessed March 12, 2012).

The media-watchdog group Media Matters, which documented this disparity in coverage, reminded its readers that Congress had planned for some failures with the Department of Energy loan guarantee program (which was actually set up before President Obama's time) because it was a portfolio of risky investments

they were making to help launch some new energy companies, and they had
set aside $2.4 billion for the cost of defaults.

"Right-Wing Media Play with Numbers, Claim DOE Loan Guarantees
Will Cost '$23 Million Per Job,'" *Media Matters,* September 29, 2011, http://
mediamatters.org/mobile/research/201109290031 (accessed March 12, 2012).

It is currently estimated that here in the United States oil companies are receiving $7,610 per minute in tax breaks—that's $4 billion per year.

"The Obama Energy Agenda: Gas Prices," White House website, http://
www.whitehouse.gov/energy/gasprices?utm_source=wh.gov&utm_
medium=shorturl&utm_campaign=shorturl (accessed March 12, 2012).

You can quibble over numbers, but fossil-fuel subsidies far outweigh those for
renewable energy. The Environmental Law Institute reckons that the US government gave more than $70 billion worth of subsidies to fossil-fuel companies
between 2002 and 2008. In that time, about $2 billion went to the solar industry.

Christian Kjaer, "More Than $5 Fossil Fuel Subsidies for Every $1 of Support for
Renewables," EWEA Blog, November 9, 2010, http://blog.ewea.org/2010/11/
more-than-5-fossil-fuel-subsidies-for-every-1-of-support-for-renewables
(accessed March 12, 2012).

US Congressman Earl Blumenauer calculates that the government is committed
to spending more than $40 billion to subsidize the fossil-fuel industry from 2011
to 2015, while no more than $10 billion is scheduled to flow into renewable-
energy businesses.

Nick Gass, "Rep. Blumenauer: Ending Big Oil Tax Incentives a 'Win-Win,'"
ABC News, April 25, 2011, http://abcnews.go.com/blogs/politics/2011/04/
rep-blumenauer-ending-big-oil-tax-incentives-a-win-win (accessed March
12, 2012).

And since the mid-2000s it's been shedding jobs; indeed, Big Oil downsized its
workforce by more than 10,000 in the second half of this century's first decade.

"Profits and Pink Slips: How Big Oil and Gas Companies Are Not Creating
US Jobs or Paying Their Fair Share," US House Natural Resources Committee
Democrats, September 8, 2011, http://democrats.naturalresources.house.gov/
content/files/2011-09-08_RPT_OilProfitsPinkSlips.pdf (accessed March 12,
2012).

For example, in California, the major market for the Rooftop Revolution so far
in the States, rebates have fallen from more than $2 per watt of solar power
installed to less than $0.50 in most utility territories.

Go Solar California/California Solar Initiative, http://www.gosolarcalifornia
.org/csi/rebates.php (accessed March 12, 2012).

As the IEA writes, "Only a small proportion should be considered subsidies or, rather, learning investments required to bring solar technologies to competitiveness."

> Giles Parkinson, "IEA Sees a World Run on Solar," *Climate Spectator,* December 6, 2011, http://www.climatespectator.com.au/commentary/iea-sees-world -run-solar (accessed March 12, 2012).

This has been well modeled in New York State, where energy regulators worked out that 5,000 megawatts of solar panels spread around the state would relieve some of the stress on the grid during times of peak demand—for example, in midsummer when air-conditioners are turned up full throttle and the state's requirement can approach 34,000 megawatts, causing frequent brownouts.

> Times Union Editorial Board, "A Bright Idea for Solar Energy," *TimesUnion. com,* January 29, 2012, http://blog.timesunion.com/opinion/a-bright-idea -%E2%80%A8for-solar-energy/17630 (accessed March 12, 2012).

David Mills, founder of the solar-plus-storage company Ausra, has shown that by using storage you can easily correlate more than 90 percent hourly grid load and hourly solar plant performance.

> "Study: Solar Thermal Power Could Supply over 90 Percent of US Grid plus Auto Fleet," Ausra, March 6, 2008, http://ausra.com/news/releases/080306 .html (accessed March 12, 2012).

The IEA says that solar power with storage is expected to be available to deliver competitive electricity globally by about 2030.

> Giles Parkinson, "IEA Sees a World Run on Solar," *Climate Spectator,* December 6, 2011, http://www.climatespectator.com.au/commentary/iea-sees-world -run-solar (accessed March 12, 2012).

The Rural Electrification Administration, which took America from having just 15 percent of homes being electrified in 1935 to 85 percent by 1950, is a model for how we can do it.

> Rural Electrification Administration, *New Deal 2.0, A Project of the Franklin and Eleanor Roosevelt Institute,* February 25, 2011, http://www.newdeal20 .org/2011/02/25/rural-electrification-administration-36317 (accessed March 12, 2012).

Big banks like HSBC, the "world's local bank," are starting to put red circles around a lot of fossil-fuel-based energy infrastructures because they may be stranded assets in the not-too-distant future.

> Giles Parkinson, "Will the Bankers Kill King Coal?" *Climate Spectator,* November 11, 2011, http://www.climatespectator.com.au/commentary/will -bankers-kill-king-coal (accessed March 12, 2012).

Climate Spectator's Giles Parkinson, one of my favorite business writers on this stuff, summarized HSBC's analysis of the speed at which clean energy can provide economic solutions. It notes, in particular, the impending arrival of wholesale prices for electricity from solar panels in India that are at or below the price per kilowatt-hour of coal-based electricity.

> Giles Parkinson, "Will the Bankers Kill King Coal?" *Climate Spectator*, November 11, 2011, http://www.climatespectator.com.au/commentary/will -bankers-kill-king-coal (accessed March 12, 2012).

In fact, going solar by 2015 will be economically rational for two-thirds of the households in the United States.

> Paul Denham, Robert M. Margolis, Sean Ong, and Billy Roberts, "Break-Even Cost for Residential Photovoltaics in the United States: Key Drivers and Sensitivities," National Renewable Energy Laboratory, December 2009, http:// www.nrel.gov/docs/fy10osti/46909.pdf (accessed March 12, 2012).

Two academics at Stanford University showed this virality with solar systems through a study of their installation in different ZIP codes.

> Bryan Bollinger and Kenneth Gillingham, "Peer Effects in the Diffusion of Solar Photovoltaic Panels," December 20, 2011, http://www.yale.edu/ gillingham/BollingerGillingham_PeerEffectsSolar.pdf (accessed March 12, 2012).

Chapter 5: Hot Jobs

What's more, these businesses now exist in all 50 states.

> Solar Energy Industries Association, http://www.solarworksforamerica.com/ States (accessed March 12, 2012).

In 2010 we had a net surplus of $2 billion in solar products traded globally. We were even a net exporter to China, the world's solar giant, by more than $240 million.

> "US Solar Energy Trade Assessment 2011: Trade Flows and Domestic Content for Solar Energy–Related Goods and Services in the United States," GTM Research Study, August 2011, http://www.seia.org/galleries/pdf/GTM -SEIA_U.S._Solar_Energy_Trade_Balance_2011.pdf (accessed March 12, 2012).

Despite a lack of sustained government support in the past decade, the overall advanced-energy economy—including wind, energy efficiency (like insulation and weather stripping), and solar—has added more than 770,000 jobs.

> Alexis Madrigal, "Green Jobs Grow: 770,000 Americans Already Have One," *Wired Science*, June 10, 2009, http://www.wired.com/wiredscience/2009/06/

green-jobs-grow-770000-americans-already-have-one (accessed March 12, 2012).

It has truly been a success: as of the end of 2011, the 1603 Treasury Program has financed more than 22,000 solar projects around the country, totaling $1.5 billion, which drove more than $3.5 billion in private investments in 47 states.

Jennifer Runyon, "Renewable Energy Groups Seek 1603 Extension; Analysts Offer Hope for Life after the Grant," *RenewableEnergyWorld.com*, December 2, 2011, http://www.renewableenergyworld.com/rea/news/article/2011/12/renewable-energy-groups-seek-1603-extension-analysts-offers-hope-for-life-after-the-grant (accessed March 12, 2012).

A survey of the US Partnership for Renewable Energy Finance estimates that the end of the cash grant program will shrink the total financing available for solar projects by 52 percent in 2012 alone—just as the demand for solar is increasing.

Jennifer Runyon, "Renewable Energy Groups Seek 1603 Extension; Analysts Offer Hope for Life after the Grant," *RenewableEnergyWorld.com*, December 2, 2011, http://www.renewableenergyworld.com/rea/news/article/2011/12/renewable-energy-groups-seek-1603-extension-analysts-offers-hope-for-life-after-the-grant (accessed March 12, 2012).

LinkedIn, which has some of the richest data about career paths and opportunities, was asked to analyze its 7 million US members who have switched industries during the past five years. The growth in the "Renewables and the Environment" category was 56.8 percent—almost off the chart. The Internet, online publishing, and wireless technology were the next closest, but these fields didn't beat 30 percent growth.

Adam Davidson, "The Economic Rebound: It Isn't What You Think, *Wired*, May 31, 2011, http://www.wired.com/magazine/2011/05/ff_jobsessay (accessed March 12, 2012).

As of 2012, 114 megawatts of solar systems are already installed in California public-sector buildings, such as schools and government offices as well as other state-run facilities, and another 239 megawatts of applications are in process. The savings to California is greater than $1.3 billion! In a state that has a $5 billion deficit, you can see the relative significance of the savings created by going solar. Schools are among the worst hit by the state's budget crisis, and a bright light for them is the savings they can realize by going solar. Of this savings, more than $800 million is expected to go to school districts and universities, freeing up resources to retain teachers and dampen budget cuts currently in process.

"Energy from Solar Panels Is Expected to Save $2.7 Million in Electricity Costs and Help Save the Environment," *Greenjobs.com*, February 2, 2012, http://www.greenjobs.com/pg/news/industrynews/industrynewsarticle.aspx?id=inews11816 (accessed March 12, 2012).

In an analysis of the literature on the subject, academics at UC Berkeley determined that renewable-energy technologies create more jobs per average megawatt of power generated and per dollar invested in construction, manufacturing, and installation than does the processing of coal or natural gas.

Max Wei, Shana Patadia, and Dan Kammen, "Putting Renewables and Energy Efficiency to Work: How Many Jobs Can the Clean Energy Industry Generate in the US?" RAEL Report, University of California, Berkeley, January 2010, http://socrates.berkeley.edu/~rael/papers.html (accessed March 12, 2012).

At around the same time that Solyndra went bust in late 2011, GE announced plans to buy a startup solar manufacturer and build a factory using its technology.

Todd Woody, "GE Buys Stake in Solar Power Plant Builder eSolar, Licenses Technology," *Forbes,* June 6, 2011, http://www.forbes.com/sites/todd woody/2011/06/06/ge-buys-stake-in-solar-power-plant-builder-esolar -licenses-technology (accessed March 12, 2012).

"We are all in. We are going to invest what it takes . . . because we know that by 2020 this is going to be at least a $1 billion product line." This was said by GE's Jeff Immelt (who also happens to head Obama's Jobs Council). "I don't care about Solyndra or any of that other stuff; we did this with no government funding. We can do this."

Scott Malone, "GE's Immelt Worries US Not Leading on Renewables," *Reuters,* November 3, 2011, http://www.reuters.com/article/2011/11/03/ge-solar -idUSN1E7A20AD20111103 (accessed March 12, 2012).

We know that the people want them: for four consecutive years, nine out of 10 Americans have said they "think it is important" for the United States to develop and use solar energy."

"New Poll: 9 out of 10 Americans Support Solar, Across Political Spectrum," Solar Energy Industries Association, November 1, 2011, http://www.seia.org/ cs/news_detail?pressrelease.id=1710 (accessed March 12, 2012).

The *Wired* magazine article "The Economic Rebound: It Isn't What You Think" analyzed job creation coming out of the recession. The publication concluded that the economy is not just gaining jobs as it slowly rebounds but also creating a new category of middle-class work that it called "smart jobs."

Adam Davidson, "The Economic Rebound: It Isn't What You Think," *Wired,* May 31, 2011, http://www.wired.com/magazine/2011/05/ff_jobsessay (accessed March 12, 2012).

This kind of business is booming—ePropser and Lending Club, which are peer-to-peer lending variations on the theme, each move hundreds of millions of dollars per year.

Matthew Paulson, "Lending Club Surpasses $500 Million in Loan Originations, Prosper Tops $300 Million," *P2P Lending News,* February 1, 2012, http://www

.p2plendingnews.com/2012/02/lending-club-surpasses-500-million-in-loan
-originations-prosper-tops-300-million (accessed March 12, 2012).

As Republican Senator Scott Brown of Massachusetts said in Congress in late 2011, crowdfunding "has the potential to be a powerful new venture capital model for the Facebook and Twitter age and its potential to create jobs is enormous."

"Sen. Brown Testifies on Crowdfunding before Banking Committee," Scott Brown, United States Senator for Massachusetts, December 1, 2011, http://www.scottbrown.senate.gov/public/index.cfm/2011/12/sen-brown-testifies-on-crowdfunding-before-banking-committee (accessed March 12, 2012).

Chapter 6: Energized

GE chief Jeff Immelt thinks India and China alone will install 200 gigawatts of solar power.

Scott Malone, "GE's Immelt Worries US Not Leading on Renewables," *Reuters*, November 3, 2011, http://www.reuters.com/article/2011/11/03/ge-solar-idUSN1E7A20AD20111103 (accessed March 12, 2012).

By 2014 the industry expects to produce 25 gigawatts of manufacturing capacity of solar panels each year.

Sungevity internal industry analysis.

In the United States, the productivity of coal mines peaked in 2000 and has decreased rapidly since.

US Energy Information Administration, "Annual Energy Review 2009" (Figure 40), http://www.eia.gov/totalenergy/data/annual/pdf/perspectives_2009 .pdf; Annual Coal Report (Table 21), http://www.eia.gov/coal/annual/pdf/ table21.pdf; and Bureau of Land Management, "Casper Field Office NEPA Documents," http://www.blm.gov/pgdata/content/wy/en/info/NEPA/ documents/cfo.html (accessed March 12, 2012).

This is the model of the carbon tax that Australia is imposing: take $20 per ton of carbon dioxide produced and create a fund to support clean energy over time.

James Grubel, "Australia Passes Landmark Carbon Price Laws," *Reuters*, November 8, 2011, http://www.reuters.com/article/2011/11/08/us-australia -carbon-idUSTRE7A60PO20111108 (accessed March 12, 2012).

Since 1992, according to the UN report "Keeping Track of Our Changing Environment," the historic rate of solar growth (30,000 percent) has actually exceeded that of Internet (29,000 percent) and cell phone (23,000 percent)

adoption, which is why I am confident that the true takeoff of the technology has only just begun.

"Keeping Track of Our Changing Environment: From Rio to Rio+20 (1992–2012)," United Nations Environment Programme, October 2011, http://www.unep.org/geo/pdfs/Keeping_Track.pdf (accessed March 12, 2012).

In 2010 three times as much solar-power capacity as nuclear-power-plant capacity was installed worldwide.

Zachary Shahan, "Renewable Energy Passed Up Nuclear in 2010," *Clean-Technica,* April 17, 2011, http://cleantechnica.com/2011/04/17/renewable-energy-passed-up-nuclear-in-2010 (accessed March 12, 2012).

For example, $88 billion is paid from the budgets of 11 of the world's poorest countries for kerosene and diesel subsidies, according to the IEA and the International Institute for Sustainable Development.

"A Look Forward to 2012 from the Carbon War Room," *Carbon War Room News & Analysis,* January 3, 2012, http://news.carbonwarroom.com/2012/01/03/a-look-forward-to-2012-from-carbon-war-room (accessed March 12, 2012).

"Solar is going to play a huge role in improving energy access," says Fatih Birol, the chief economist at the IEA.

Bryan Walsh, "The Worst Kind of Poverty: Energy Poverty," *Time,* http://www.time.com/time/health/article/0,8599,2096602,00.html (accessed March 12, 2012).

At least $2 trillion to $5 trillion will be spent on energy worldwide in the coming two decades.

"The High Cost of Fossil Fuels," Environment America, June 30, 2009, http://www.environmentamerica.org/reports/ame/high-cost-fossil-fuels; and "Spending on New Renewable Energy Capacity to Total $7 Trillion over Next 20 Years," *Bloomberg New Energy Finance,* November 16, 2011, http://bnef.com/PressReleases/view/173 (accessed March 12, 2012).

The DOD's clean-energy investments grew more than 300 percent from 2006 to 2009 and are projected to continue at that clip through 2030.

Pew Project on National Security, Energy and Climate, "From Barracks to the Battlefield: Clean Energy Innovation and America's Armed Forces," Pew Environment Group, September 21, 2011, http://www.pewenvironment.org/news-room/reports/from-barracks-to-battlefield-clean-energy-innovation-and-americas-armed-forces-85899364060 (accessed March 12, 2012).

You might be surprised to know that some of the highest casualty rates among our troops in the past decade were sustained while protecting diesel shipments

used to air-condition tents in our foreign wars; and the greatest risks of war to date with more countries relate to petroleum or nuclear power, from North Korea to Iran.

> Nick Hodge, "Energy in 2030," *Energy and Capital,* October 15, 2011, http://www.energyandcapital.com/articles/energy-in-2030/1837 (accessed March 12, 2012).

Epilogue: Fire 2.0 *My Ride on the Solar Coaster—So Far*

This model has been so wildly successful that it has gone from no market share just four years ago to being the majority of the residential solar market in the United States today. By the end of 2011, third-party-financed systems were 60 percent of the home solar market.

> "Sunrun and PV Solar Report Announce Solar Leasing Has Eclipsed Cash Purchases," *Sunrun,* October 17, 2011, http://www.sunrunhome.com/about-sunrun/sunrun-in-the-news/2012-press-releases/sunrun-and-pv-solar-report-announce-solar-leasing-has-eclipsed-cash-purchases (accessed March 12, 2012).

Recently, I came across a definition of *entrepreneurship* on Inc.com: "the pursuit of opportunity without regard to resources currently controlled."

> Eric Schurenberg, "What's an Entrepreneur? The Best Answer Ever," *Inc.,* January 9, 2012, http://www.inc.com/eric-schurenberg/the-best-definition-of-entepreneurship.html (accessed March 12, 2012).

Additional Resources

José A. Alfonso, "BP Solar Abandons Solar Power," *Renewable Energy Magazine,* December 19, 2011, http://www.renewableenergymagazine.com/energias/ renovables/index/pag/pv_solar/colleft/colright/pv_solar/tip/articulo/ pagid/18390/botid/71 (accessed March 12, 2012).

An Inconvenient Truth, produced and directed by Davis Guggenheim, featuring Al Gore (Los Angeles: Paramount 2006), DVD.

A Road Not Taken, produced and directed by Christina Hemauer and Roman Keller (2010, Hemauer | Keller), DVD.

Bryan Bollinger and Kenneth Gillingham, "Peer Effects in the Diffusion of Solar Photovoltaic Panels," December 20, 2011, http://www.yale.edu/gillingham/ BollingerGillingham_PeerEffectsSolar.pdf (accessed March 12, 2012).

Paul Denham, Robert M. Margolis, Sean Ong, and Billy Roberts, "Break-Even Cost for Residential Photovoltaics in the United States: Key Drivers and Sensitivities," National Renewable Energy Laboratory, December 2009, http:// www.nrel.gov/docs/fy10osti/46909.pdf (accessed March 12, 2012).

Electrification Coalition, *Electrification Roadmap: Revolutionizing Transportation and Achieving Energy Security,* November 2009, http://www .electrificationcoalition.org/sites/default/files/SAF_1213_EC-Roadmap_v12_ Online.pdf (accessed March 12, 2012).

Barbara Freese, *Coal: A Human History* (Cambridge, MA: Perseus, 2003).

"Germany Generates 60% More Solar Electricity in 2011," *Energy Matters,* January 2, 2012, http://www.energymatters.com.au/index.php?main_page=news_ article&article_id=1960 (accessed March 12, 2012).

"Koch Brothers, Grover Norquist Split on Ethanol Subsidies," Ryan Grimm, *Huffington Post,* August 13, 2011, http://www.huffingtonpost.com/2011/06/13/ koch-brothers-ethanol-subsidies-grover-norquist_n_876430.html (accessed March 12, 2012)."Jobs in Renewable Energy Expanding," *Worldwatch Institute,*

ROOFTOP REVOLUTION

http://www.worldwatch.org/node/5821 (last modified February 20, 2012; accessed March 12, 2012). "Keeping Track of Our Changing Environment: From Rio to Rio+20 (1992–2012)," United Nations Environment Programme, October 2011, http://www.unep.org/geo/pdfs/Keeping_Track.pdf (accessed March 12, 2012).

Jeremy Leggett, *The Empty Tank: Oil, Gas, Hot Air, and the Coming Global Financial Catastrophe* (New York: Random House, 2005).

Bill Moyers, JoAnn McAllister, Mary Lou Finley, and Steven Soifer, *Doing Democracy: The MAP Model for Organizing Social Movements* (Gabriola Island, BC, Canada: New Society Publishers, 2001).

Ramez Naam, "Smaller, Cheaper, Faster: Does Moore's Law Apply to Solar Cells?" *Scientific American,* March 16, 2011, http://blogs.scientificamerican.com/guest -blog/2011/03/16/smaller-cheaper-faster-does-moores-law-apply-to-solar -cells (accessed March 12, 2012).

Giles Parkinson, "Will the Bankers Kill King Coal?" *Climate Spectator,* November 11, 2011, http://www.climatespectator.com.au/commentary/will-bankers-kill -king-coal (accessed March 12, 2012).

Cédric Philibert, "Solar Energy Perspectives," International Energy Agency World Solar Congress, September 1, 2011, www.iea.org/speech/2011/solar_ perspectives.pdf (accessed March 12, 2012).

Renewable Energy Policy Network for the 21st Century, *Renewables 2011 Global Status Report,* November 2011, http://www.worldwatch.org/node/8588 (accessed March 12, 2012).

Bryan Walsh, "The Worst Kind of Poverty: Energy Poverty," *Time,* October 11, 2011, http://www.time.com/time/health/article/0,8599,2096602,00 .html#ixzz1iYYavTWu (accessed March 12, 2012).

Acknowledgments

I NEVER IMAGINED I'D WRITE A BOOK, BUT A BUNCH OF PEOPLE compelled me to do so, and I am truly grateful to them and all the people I have represented in these pages. So, to start, I should thank my wonderfully talented collaborator and co-writer, Robert Ordona, and our ever-vigilant project manager, John Ordona, for making this book a reality. You both rock! I'm also grateful to Charles Purdy for his masterful editorial feedback and his generous collaboration, and to Elsa Dixon for helping launch this project.

The reason I had not been too keen on writing a book is that I am a big believer in deeds over words. And yet, as my publisher Neal Maillet and the great people at Berrett-Koehler have shown me, a good book can be a way to propel a movement. Just as the technology of the printing press propelled the rise of the steam age—thus spurring the Industrial Revolution—I'm hoping this book can spur a Rooftop Revolution brought by the rise of new information and energy technologies.

So, thank you, Neal and the Berrett-Koehler team, for your support and partnership.

Another reason I never wanted to write a book was that I'd have to sit down and think of all the people whose ideas I've stolen and then acknowledge them and their influence on me. I don't mind having stolen from them—I just hope they don't!

And it makes me a little too nostalgic to think of all the great people who have helped me along the way and whom I have rarely followed up with to let them know how appreciative I am. I see now that we really are standing on others' shoulders when we reach any height. So here's my shot at shouting out a heartfelt thanks to those whose shoulders have been solid enough to hold me.

First up, let me say that my family and community are the biggest, best influence on me. Mum and Dad, Boo and Tinny— you were wonderful to grow up with (as much as I did). Now I love growing old with my own family and the "Orchardistas." Thanks for keeping it real and fun while keeping us all focused on a better place.

I have to thank Harvey and all the Greenpeacers over the years who helped me see that King CONG is an emperor without clothes and who taught me to have some fun exposing his nudity. Nic, Iain, Val, Roz, Jeremy, Gary, Lena, Pene, Bunny, Hepburn, Passacantando, JP, Catherine, Sze Ping, Bruno, Sawyer, Sven, Sonia, and so many others—I salute you.

Ken Saro Wiwa and the wonderful people of Oilwatch International, the Movement for the Survival of the Ogoni People, and the Indigenous Environmental Network—like Ken Jr. and his brother Owens, plus Oronto, Esperanza, Steve, Randy, Red, Terry, Atossa, Gopal, Goat, Walt, Tom, Pratap, Charoen, and others who connected me to the work against extreme energy extraction—I honor you all. May you succeed in your struggles to create a better world.

Going back even farther into the mists of my mind, there are many student activists who gave me a sense of ire and satire that helps me stay sane when dealing with the insanely inefficient world of electricity in the United States today. The Student

Environmental Action Coalition and the Young Turks of Action for Solidarity, Equality, Environment, and Development back in the 1980s and 1990s, who taught me most of what I know about making social change—especially Miya, my wife and wonderful guide in this thing called life.

Finally, for those who share my enterprise of selling sunshine, which is so much fun, I have to thank all the people who make up Sungevity and all the people who gave me courage to get the company going with Birchy and Alec—first among them, Birchy and Alec! But also Cate and Andrew, Tara and Warwick, the Guettel family, Claire, Doug, Dan, Dr. Shi, Gavin, Cathy and Kantau, and many others.

Alongside the SFUNsters, there are others working to achieve the vision of solar for universal need. I am grateful that even when we compete for business we have a bigger purpose as an industry and appreciate everyone, from Nick to David, Svea to Roeby, and all the good solar folk in between who are striving to make it mainstream and universal.

There's much more to be said of all of these people, and there are twice as many folk whom I have failed to mention. For now may those of you who think you should have been mentioned, please know that I appreciate all that you have taught me. For everyone else reading this, I'm grateful to have an audience and hope to see you out there on the rooftops!

Index

About the Author

DANNY KENNEDY IS A GLOBAL AUTHOR-ity on environmental issues and a successful clean-tech entrepreneur. His accomplishments have earned him numerous awards, including Innovator of the Year by PBS's Planet Forward for pioneering an easy-to-access and affordable residential solar solution.

Kennedy has worked on climate and energy issues for more than two decades.

At Greenpeace he initially focused on ending new oil exploration in the Pacific; and as the leader of the organization's California Clean Energy Now campaign, he helped create the state's solar policies, which provide substantial market support for solar businesses and help Golden State citizens go solar. In 1996 Kennedy founded and directed Project Underground, an organization committed to protecting the human rights of people abused and exploited by mining and oil operations.

In 2007 Kennedy founded Sungevity Inc., which has become a leading residential solar-power company. He serves as Sungevity's president and oversees government relations and community engagement programs.

Tireless in his efforts to evangelize the mass adoption of solar power, Kennedy serves on the boards of The Solar Foundation, a global research and education organization in Washington, DC, and Solar Mosaic, a solar-focused, crowdfunding startup in Oakland, California.

Kennedy lives in the San Francisco Bay Area with his wife, Miya Yoshitani, their two daughters, and seven chickens.

About Sungevity

The Sungevity co-founders at one of their countless weekend work sessions (left to right): Alec Guettel, chairman; Danny Kennedy, president; and Andrew "Birchy" Birch, CEO

FOUNDED IN 2007, SUNGEVITY IS ONE OF THE WORLD'S LEADing residential solar-energy companies. Leveraging web-based solar analytics and satellite imagery, the company's online iQuote process—combined with its solar lease program—provides homeowners with an easy and affordable solar-energy solution. Based in Oakland, California, Sungevity provides solar services in a growing number of US states and is the exclusive residential solar partner for Lowe's, one of the world's largest home-improvement retailers.

In 2011 Sungevity expanded to Europe through a partnership with Dutch company Zonline to provide residential solar service to the people of the Netherlands. In 2012 Sungevity formed a joint venture with Nickel Energy to launch Sungevity Australia.

For more information visit www.sungevity.com.

Berrett–Koehler
Publishers

Berrett-Koehler is an independent publisher dedicated to an ambitious mission: *Creating a World That Works for All*.

We believe that to truly create a better world, action is needed at all levels—individual, organizational, and societal. At the individual level, our publications help people align their lives with their values and with their aspirations for a better world. At the organizational level, our publications promote progressive leadership and management practices, socially responsible approaches to business, and humane and effective organizations. At the societal level, our publications advance social and economic justice, shared prosperity, sustainability, and new solutions to national and global issues.

A major theme of our publications is "Opening Up New Space." Berrett-Koehler titles challenge conventional thinking, introduce new ideas, and foster positive change. Their common quest is changing the underlying beliefs, mindsets, institutions, and structures that keep generating the same cycles of problems, no matter who our leaders are or what improvement programs we adopt.

We strive to practice what we preach—to operate our publishing company in line with the ideas in our books. At the core of our approach is stewardship, which we define as a deep sense of responsibility to administer the company for the benefit of all of our "stakeholder" groups: authors, customers, employees, investors, service providers, and the communities and environment around us.

We are grateful to the thousands of readers, authors, and other friends of the company who consider themselves to be part of the "BK Community." We hope that you, too, will join us in our mission.

A BK Currents Book

This book is part of our BK Currents series. BK Currents books advance social and economic justice by exploring the critical intersections between business and society. Offering a unique combination of thoughtful analysis and progressive alternatives, BK Currents books promote positive change at the national and global levels. To find out more, visit **www.bkconnection.com**.

Berrett–Koehler
Publishers

A community dedicated to creating
a world that works for all

Visit Our Website: www.bkconnection.com

Read book excerpts, see author videos and Internet movies, read
our authors' blogs, join discussion groups, download book apps, find
out about the BK Affiliate Network, browse subject-area libraries of
books, get special discounts, and more!

Subscribe to Our Free E-Newsletter, the *BK Communiqué*

Be the first to hear about new publications, special discount offers,
exclusive articles, news about bestsellers, and more! Get on the list
for our free e-newsletter by going to **www.bkconnection.com**.

Get Quantity Discounts

Berrett-Koehler books are available at quantity discounts for orders
of ten or more copies. Please call us toll-free at (800) 929-2929 or
email us at bkp.orders@aidcvt.com.

Join the BK Community

BKcommunity.com is a virtual meeting place where people from
around the world can engage with kindred spirits to create a world
that works for all. BKcommunity.com members may create their own
profiles, blog, start and participate in forums and discussion groups,
post photos and videos, answer surveys, announce and register for
upcoming events, and chat with others online in real time. Please join
the conversation!